THE WILD HISTORY OF THE AMERICAN WEST

THE
LOUISIANA PURCHASE
—THE DEAL OF THE CENTURY
THAT DOUBLED THE NATION

David Schaffer

MyReportLinks.com Books

an imprint of

 Enslow Publishers, Inc.

Box 398, 40 Industrial Road
Berkeley Heights, NJ 07922
USA

To Dad, my first history teacher

MyReportLinks.com Books, an imprint of Enslow Publishers, Inc. MyReportLinks®
is a registered trademark of Enslow Publishers, Inc.

Copyright © 2006 by Enslow Publishers, Inc.

Library of Congress Cataloging-in-Publication Data

Schaffer, David, 1960–
  The Louisiana Purchase : the deal of the century that doubled the nation / David Schaffer.
     p. cm. — (The wild history of the American West)
  Includes bibliographical references and index.
  ISBN 1-59845-018-2
  1. Louisiana Purchase—Juvenile literature. 2. United States—History—1801–1809—
Juvenile literature. 3. Napoleon I, Emperor of the French, 1769–1821—Relations with
Americans—Juvenile literature. 4. United States—Territorial expansion—Juvenile
literature. I. Title. II. Series.
  E333.S33 2006
  973.4'6—dc22

                                    2005033172

Printed in the United States of America

10 9 8 7 6 5 4 3 2 1

To Our Readers:
Through the purchase of this book, you and your library gain access to the Report Links that specifically back
up this book.

The Publisher will provide access to the Report Links that back up this book and will keep these Report Links
up to date on **www.myreportlinks.com** for five years from the book's first publication date.

We have done our best to make sure all Internet addresses in this book were active and appropriate when we
went to press. However, the author and the Publisher have no control over, and assume no liability for, the mate-
rial available on those Internet sites or on other Web sites they may link to.

The usage of the MyReportLinks.com Books Web site is subject to the terms and conditions stated on the Usage
Policy Statement on **www.myreportlinks.com.**

A password may be required to access the Report Links that back up this book. The password is found on the
bottom of page 4 of this book.

Any comments or suggestions can be sent by e-mail to comments@myreportlinks.com or to the address on the
back cover.

CONTENTS

MyReportLinks.com Books
Great Books, Great Links, Great for Research!

The Internet sites featured in this book can save you hours of research time. These Internet sites—we call them **"Report Links"**—are constantly changing, but we keep them up to date on our Web site.

When you see this "Approved Web Site" logo, you will know that we are directing you to a great Internet site that will help you with your research.

Give it a try! Type http://www.myreportlinks.com into your browser, click on the series title and enter the password, then click on the book title, and scroll down to the Report Links listed for this book.

The Report Links will bring you to great source documents, photographs, and illustrations. MyReportLinks.com Books save you time, feature Report Links that are kept up to date, and make report writing easier than ever! A complete listing of the Report Links can be found on pages 118–119 at the back of the book.

Please see "To Our Readers" on the copyright page for important information about this book, the MyReportLinks.com Web site, and the Report Links that back up this book.

Please enter **WLP1137** if asked for a password.

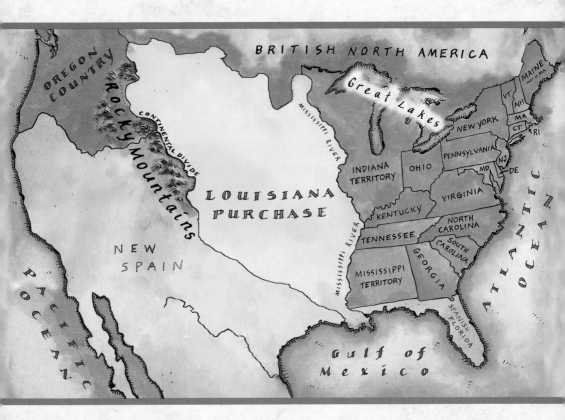

▲ Map of the Louisiana Purchase territory and the United States in 1803.

LOUISIANA PURCHASE TIME LINE

▷ **CA 1000 –800 B.C.** — The Mississippian civilization developed along the banks of the Mississippi River.

▷ **A.D. 1541** — Hernando de Soto led the first Spanish expedition across the Mississippi River.

▷ **1673** — Louis Jolliet and Jacques Marquette became the first Frenchmen to explore the Mississippi River and Valley.

▷ **1682** — René-Robert Cavelier, Sieur de La Salle, traveled the full length of the Mississippi, named the territory in the eastern and western basins Louisiana, and claimed the entire territory for France.

▷ **1699** — First permanent French settlement in Louisiana is established.

▷ **1754 –1763** — The French and Indian War; France is defeated. Ceded eastern Louisiana Territory to Great Britain; Western territory and New Orleans to Spain.

▷ **1775 –1783** — The American Revolutionary War; Afterward, the United States gained the eastern Louisiana Territory.

▷ **1784** — The Spanish banned foreign trade in lower Mississippi and New Orleans.

▷ **1789 –1799** — The French Revolution deposed the monarchy and eventually brought Napoléon to absolute power in France.

▷ **1795** — The Treaty of San Lorenzo restored trading rights for Americans on the Mississippi River and in New Orleans.

▷ **1800** — The Treaty of San Ildefonso between Spain and France secretly returned New Orleans and Louisiana to France.

▷ **1801** — Robert Livingston arrived in Paris to begin negotiations over the purchase of New Orleans and Louisiana with Charles-Maurice de Talleyrand-Périgord and Francois Barbé-Marbois. Livingston is soon joined by James Monroe.

▷ **1803**—Agreement reached between the United States and France on the purchase of Louisiana and New Orleans; Lower Louisiana is officially turned over to the United States.

▷ **1804**—The United States took possession of upper Louisiana; The territories are divided into Orleans Territory and Louisiana Territory; Meriwether Lewis and William Clark began their western expedition, leading the Corps of Discovery.

▷ **1805** —Aaron Burr and James Wilkinson schemed to lead the western ter-
—**1806** ritories into secession and start a new nation; Wilkinson betrayed Burr and gave the plot away.

▷ **1810**—The United States seized part of the western Florida territory, claiming it is part of Orleans.

▷ **1812**—Orleans Territory is admitted to the United States as the state of Louisiana; The War of 1812 broke out between Great Britain and the United States.

▷ **1814**—Treaty of Ghent formally ends War of 1812.

▷ **1815**—Although the war had already ended, Andrew Jackson led American troops to an overwhelming victory over the British at the Battle of New Orleans, helping to establish lasting United States domain over the western territories.

Chapter 1

ON THE BRINK OF WAR

LOUISIANA PURCHASE

As the 1700s were coming to a close, there loomed the threat of a major war between France, one of the leading military powers of the world, and the newly formed United States. France was led by Napoléon Bonaparte, ruler and conqueror. Napoléon had established an empire in Europe and was intent on extending it to North America. One large and attractive land possession greatly interested Napoléon. This was the territory west of the Mississippi River known as the Louisiana Territory, as well as New Orleans, the port city at the southeast end of the Mississippi River. The Louisiana Territory covered a staggering 600,000 square miles. In 1803, that was about the same size as the entire United States.

Someone else was equally determined to claim the Louisiana Territory and New Orleans for his country. His name was Thomas Jefferson, the third American president, and a strong believer in American westward expansion. He believed that the United States was entitled and destined to take control of those areas. The number of

American settlers who moved to those areas from the original colonies along the east coast continued to grow.

Originally, Louisiana had been a French settlement, but the territory belonged to Spain since 1763. Spain, though, lost a great deal of power during the eighteenth century. Spanish forces were not able to stop Americans from easily passing through the territory and using its waterways. Most importantly, under Spanish rule, Americans had been permitted to store and trade goods in the port city of New Orleans. This gave them

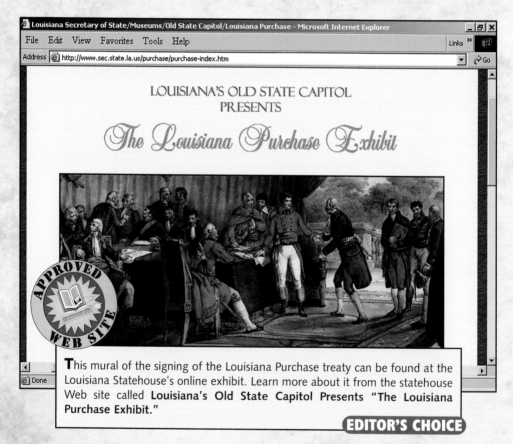

This mural of the signing of the Louisiana Purchase treaty can be found at the Louisiana Statehouse's online exhibit. Learn more about it from the statehouse Web site called **Louisiana's Old State Capitol Presents "The Louisiana Purchase Exhibit."**

direct access to shipping lanes. Jefferson was okay with Spain possessing Louisiana and New Orleans, at least for the short term. He felt differently about the possibility of France, a strong and growing military power, taking over the territory.

Word spread that Spain and France had reached a secret agreement turning Louisiana and New Orleans over to France. Jefferson was very displeased. He did not want New Orleans to become part of the French Empire. Jefferson wrote a letter to Robert Livingston, the American diplomat in France. The president boldly claimed that should this transfer take place, the United States would react, and there could be grave consequences:

Of all nations . . . France is the one which hitherto has offered the fewest points on which we could have any conflict of right, and the most points of communion of interest. [Therefore] we have ever looked to her as our *natural friend*. . . . There is on the globe one single spot, the possessor of which is our natural and habitual enemy. It is New Orleans, through which the produce of three-eighths of our territory must pass to market. . . . France placing herself in that door assumes to us the attitude of defiance. Spain might have retained it quietly for years. . . . and it would not perhaps be long before some circumstances might arise which might make the cession of it to us [worthwhile]. . . . Not so can it ever be in the hands of France. . . . The day that France takes possession of N. Orleans fixes the

New Orleans has been an important port for centuries. The variety of people coming in and out led to a great mix of cultures. There are still examples of French architecture in New Orleans today. Sadly, some of these buildings need to be rebuilt after Hurricane Katrina struck in 2005.

sentence. . . . It seals the union of two nations [the U.S. and Great Britain] who in conjunction can maintain exclusive possession of the ocean. From that moment we must marry ourselves to the British fleet and nation.[1]

Jefferson mentioned Great Britain because Great Britain and France were fierce military rivals. The British had a greater navy, and because the United States was located much closer to Louisiana and New Orleans than France, an alliance would benefit British trade. An alliance between the United States and Great Britain would have presented France with a stiff challenge over the territory.

Scrambling for a Settlement

France and the United States posed a serious war threat to each other. Yet both hoped that an agreement could be reached that would avoid war. The United States wanted to purchase New Orleans for a reasonable price and was prepared to accept French possession of the land west of the Mississippi. For its part, France planned to offer the United States the same favorable trading rights in New Orleans that it had with Spain.

Officially, the two most important people involved in the talks over New Orleans were Robert Livingston and French foreign minister Charles-Maurice de Talleyrand-Périgord. In reality, Napoléon alone determined New Orleans' fate.

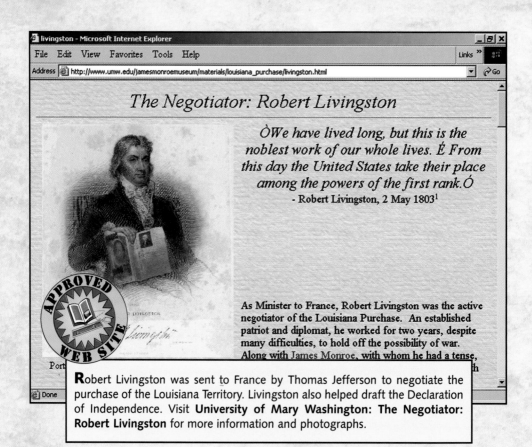

livingston - Microsoft Internet Explorer

File   Edit   View   Favorites   Tools   Help   Links »

Address http://www.umw.edu/jamesmonroemuseum/materials/louisiana_purchase/livingston.html   Go

The Negotiator: Robert Livingston

"We have lived long, but this is the noblest work of our whole lives. … From this day the United States take their place among the powers of the first rank."
- Robert Livingston, 2 May 1803[1]

As Minister to France, Robert Livingston was the active negotiator of the Louisiana Purchase. An established patriot and diplomat, he worked for two years, despite many difficulties, to hold off the possibility of war. Along with James Monroe, with whom he had a tense,

Port

Done

Robert Livingston was sent to France by Thomas Jefferson to negotiate the purchase of the Louisiana Territory. Livingston also helped draft the Declaration of Independence. Visit **University of Mary Washington: The Negotiator: Robert Livingston** for more information and photographs.

He not only decided to turn New Orleans over to the United States, but also to cede the entire Louisiana Territory to the new nation. Napoléon made the decision in the presence of only two of his highest-ranking advisors. He gave no indication to anyone else, even as discussion and speculation about who should control New Orleans went on.

As chief representative of American interests in France, Livingston tried persistently to settle the Louisiana matter with Talleyrand after receiving Jefferson's firm direction. The French minister refused to admit that Spain and France had struck a deal and he claimed that New Orleans was not France's to give away or sell. Livingston tried to talk with someone other than Talleyrand, appealing to Napoléon's brothers. He even wrote a letter directly to Napoléon. Yet Talleyrand continued to stand in the way of a deal.

New Players on the Scene

Livingston had other concerns. Another diplomat from the United States, James Monroe, had been sent by Jefferson to France to help negotiate a deal for New Orleans. Livingston was offended, although Jefferson insisted he was sending Monroe mostly as a symbolic gesture to Americans in the western territories. Monroe owned land in the West, and was preferred over Livingston by many western Americans. Many westerners feared that Jefferson and Livingston were not sympathetic to them and were not acting tough enough in the negotiations with France. Nevertheless, Livingston let his displeasure be known. In a letter to United States Secretary of State James Madison, Livingston stated that "he had established a confidence that it will take Mr. Monroe some time to inspire."[2]

Talleyrand's importance as the lead French negotiator also came to be challenged. French Finance Minister Francois Barbé-Marbois had been

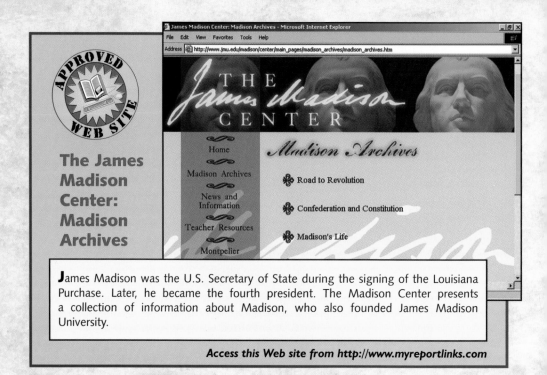

The James
Madison
Center:
Madison
Archives

James Madison Center: Madison Archives - Microsoft Internet Explorer

File   Edit   View   Favorites   Tools   Help

Address http://www.jmu.edu/madison/center/main_pages/madison_archives/madison_archives.htm

THE *James Madison* CENTER

Madison Archives

Home

Madison Archives

News and
Information

Teacher Resources

Montpelier

Road to Revolution

Confederation and Constitution

Madison's Life

James Madison was the U.S. Secretary of State during the signing of the Louisiana Purchase. Later, he became the fourth president. The Madison Center presents a collection of information about Madison, who also founded James Madison University.

Access this Web site from http://www.myreportlinks.com

one of the first people in whom Napoléon confided when he decided to sell both Louisiana and New Orleans to the United States. Barbé-Marbois had remained a firm supporter of the sale, even as others in Napoléon's inner circle expressed heavy opposition. Napoléon came to rely on Barbé-Marbois to carry out his will concerning Louisiana and New Orleans. Barbé-Marbois became the chief negotiator for the French.

Before Monroe arrived in the French capital of Paris, and before Barbé-Marbois took over for Talleyrand, Livingston and Talleyrand both tried speeding up the negotiations. They hoped to get credit for the huge land deal. On April 11, 1802,

Talleyrand called Livingston to his office. Without making any commitment, he asked Livingston how the United States might feel about purchasing not just New Orleans but also the entire Louisiana Territory. Livingston was shocked. He was not prepared for such an offer—the United States had been hoping only to acquire the port of New Orleans and, if it could, the remainder of the territory along the Gulf of Mexico.

Livingston was not authorized to purchase all of Louisiana, but he did not want to lose this chance. He suggested that the United States might be willing to pay as much as $4 million. Talleyrand dismissed the amount as far too small, but a series of intense and dramatic negotiations was set in motion.

▷ Monroe's Arrival

When pressed to make another offer for Louisiana, Livingston stalled. He claimed that James Monroe would be arriving shortly, and he needed to confer with him before discussing the matter further.

Monroe arrived at Livingston's residence the next day. While the two families dined, French finance minister Barbé-Marbois visited and asked Livingston to come to his office later that evening. It was at that point that Barbé-Marbois began to play a major role in the negotiations, replacing Talleyrand as the main French representative.

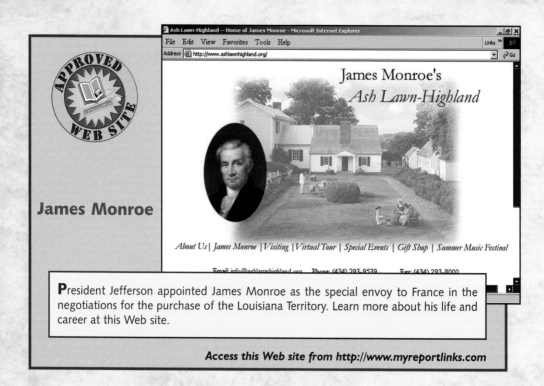

James Monroe

President Jefferson appointed James Monroe as the special envoy to France in the negotiations for the purchase of the Louisiana Territory. Learn more about his life and career at this Web site.

Access this Web site from http://www.myreportlinks.com

The meeting between Barbé-Marbois and Livingston proved fateful. Marbois hid how determined Napoléon was to sell Louisiana and New Orleans. He claimed that Napoléon had authorized him to make a deal for the territories, but for a high price—100 million francs, or about $25 million. This was much more than Livingston had offered the previous day. He still was not authorized to negotiate for the entire Louisiana Territory. Still, he realized that this was a fantastic bargain for the United States. Like Barbé-Marbois, Livingston acted cleverly, concealing his true feelings. He told Barbé-Marbois that the amount was more than the United States could afford. He reminded Barbé-Marbois that the United States had not sought all of Louisiana and did not make an offer even when asked to name a price by Barbé-Marbois. Livingston did not budge even when Barbé-Marbois dropped the price to $15 million. Once again he claimed that he needed to consult with Monroe before proceeding. As historian Thomas Fleming points out, Livingston portrayed his true feelings upon returning to his residence after the meeting: "Livingston devoted almost three hours to writing a long letter to [United States Secretary of State] James Madison, hoping to get on the record that he had all but bought Louisiana without any help from James Monroe. . . . [Livingston] had no hesitation in crowing over the bargain."[3]

▷ Closing the Deal

French and American representatives wrangled over the price of Louisiana for most of the next month. Monroe and Livingston stuck together in negotiations despite their differences. They made an offer of 40 million francs, about $10 million. Later they increased it to 50 million francs when Barbé-Marbois implied that if they were unable to settle the affair soon, the Americans might have to deal once again with the difficult and devious Talleyrand instead of himself.

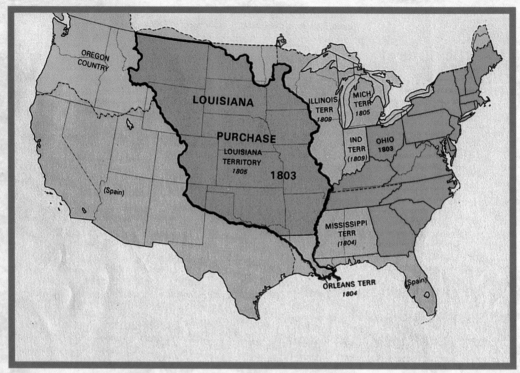

▲ This map shows the size of the United States by 1810. The Louisiana Territory is highlighted in between the two dark lines that is mostly the dark green area.

In the meantime, pressure on Napoléon to reverse his decision to sell the Louisiana Territory was increasing. His own brothers opposed the deal and threatened to lead a revolt over it. Barbé-Marbois feared Napoléon might withdraw the offer, or that he might even be replaced as ruler by those determined to keep the territory. Barbé-Marbois again issued an offer for the figure of 60 million francs, now saying that the offer was final. The Americans reluctantly agreed, not wanting to let the chance to settle the issue slip away. Monroe and Livingston also agreed to cover the cost of claims made by American merchants against France as part of the deal. This brought the total cost to the United States to $20 million.

Even this amount was a small price, considering the enormous size of the Louisiana Territory. Indeed, the Louisiana Purchase ranks among the greatest land deals ever made. The acquisition of the Louisiana Territory also proved to be an event of immeasurable importance in the growth and development of the United States.

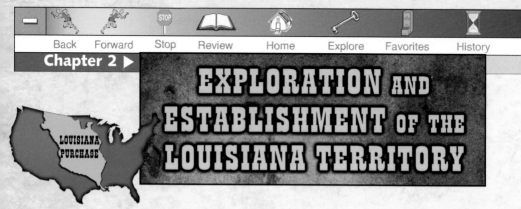

Chapter 2

EXPLORATION AND ESTABLISHMENT OF THE LOUISIANA TERRITORY

Prior to becoming a part of the United States, the area known as the Louisiana Territory was home to a variety of American Indian tribes. It was then colonized by three major European powers— Great Britain, France, and Spain. During the early years of European settlement in America, these nations competed for, and clashed over, these western frontier territories. Yet none was able to utilize the potential of the territory in the way the United States would after making the Louisiana Purchase.

▷ **American Indians in the Louisiana Territory**
Long before the first Europeans reached the western interior of America, others occupied the region. A highly advanced American Indian civilization known as the Mississippians had developed along the Mississippi Valley. The most powerful of these tribes became the Chickasaw, Choctaw, and Natchez. They had been there since at least A.D. 800. The Mississippians lived in settlements set upon elevated mounds of earth. Their cities were ruled by hereditary leaders, as were

civilizations in Europe and Central and South America. They built elaborate and ornate structures for their leaders to live in and open plazas in their town centers. Mississippians depended primarily on farming but were also skillful hunters and fishers. Their largest settlement, Cahokia, in

The Mississipian Mound Builders were a highly civilized society that created a city at Cahokia. The Mound Builders abandoned Cahokia around A.D. 800.

what is now Illinois, had a population of about ten thousand at its peak. This was the largest American Indian center anywhere north of Mexico, where the acutely skilled Aztec and Maya civilizations were based.

River Settlements and the Great Plains

The Mississippians lived primarily along the banks of the Mississippi River and other large rivers that feed into it. The land near the rivers is moist, fine, and easy to farm. These early inhabitants lacked advanced equipment such as plows, or large work animals such as horses or oxen. There were also American Indians who lived in the more distant and rugged areas of the territory, to the north and west of the Mississippian settlements. These tribes lived nomadically, moving from place to place and hunting and gathering for food and clothing. The massive buffalo herds of the Great Plains were a primary source of food and other supplies for these people. A few minor farming communities, located along smaller rivers and other remote wetlands, also existed in the Great Plains area. Corn and beans were the principal crops grown there.

It is uncertain for how long American Indians had lived in the Louisiana Territory when the first European explorers came in the mid-sixteenth century. It is likely they had been there for close to two thousand years.[1] The arrival of the Europeans

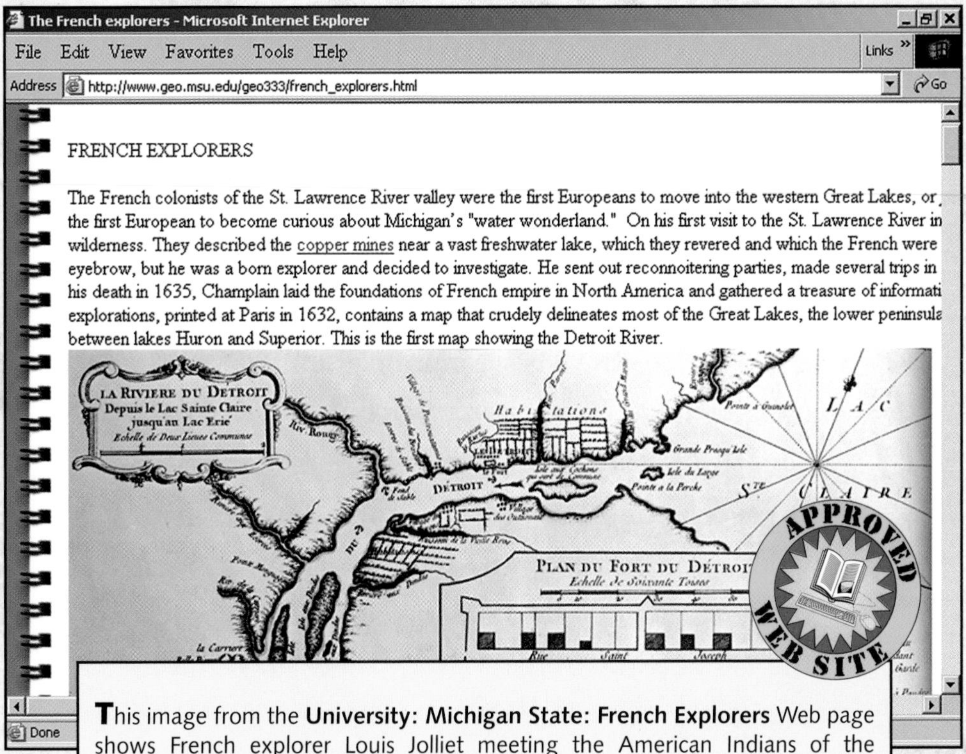
The French explorers - Microsoft Internet Explorer
File Edit View Favorites Tools Help
Address http://www.geo.msu.edu/geo333/french_explorers.html
FRENCH EXPLORERS
The French colonists of the St. Lawrence River valley were the first Europeans to move into the western Great Lakes, or
the first European to become curious about Michigan's "water wonderland." On his first visit to the St. Lawrence River in
wilderness. They described the copper mines near a vast freshwater lake, which they revered and which the French were
eyebrow, but he was a born explorer and decided to investigate. He sent out reconnoitering parties, made several trips in
his death in 1635, Champlain laid the foundations of French empire in North America and gathered a treasure of informati
explorations, printed at Paris in 1632, contains a map that crudely delineates most of the Great Lakes, the lower peninsula
between lakes Huron and Superior. This is the first map showing the Detroit River.
LA RIVIERE DU DETROIT
Depuis le Lac Sainte Claire
jusqu'au Lac Erie
DETROIT
PLAN DU FORT DU DETROIT
LAC
APPROVED WEB SITE
Done

This image from the **University: Michigan State: French Explorers** Web page shows French explorer Louis Jolliet meeting the American Indians of the Mississippi delta region.

marked a dramatic change in their lives and in the history of the territory.

Spanish Expeditions

The first Europeans to sail into the Mississippi River and explore the surrounding area were Spanish. Hernando de Soto led a group of over six hundred men on an expedition in 1539. This expedition hoped to find gold and other treasures, much like the Spanish had obtained by conquering the Aztec and Mayan civilizations to the south. The Spanish also hoped to find a water route between the Atlantic and Pacific oceans through the American continent. This was a goal that explorers of many nations would seek for years to come.

De Soto and Coronado

De Soto's expedition landed in what is now Florida, and headed west. They reached the eastern banks of the Mississippi two years later. They then crossed the river, which they called the Great River of Florida, and continued westward. However, de Soto succeeded in finding neither gold nor a passageway to the Pacific. In pursuit of these goals, de Soto's forces brutally attacked the American Indians that they encountered. According to historian Marshall Sprague, "[de Soto's] method of controlling the Indians . . . was to shoot them or starve them or wear them out in slave labor—a process of systematic inhumanity that they never forgot or forgave."[2] The Spanish lost many men fighting the American Indians. De Soto died of disease on May 21, 1542, in what is now Texas. De Soto's men returned to the Mississippi River with his body.

With provisions low, and neither of his goals achieved, his men knew they needed to return to Spanish territory. They planned to try to make their way to Mexico. Of the remaining members of the expedition, only a little over three hundred made it to Mexico in 1543. The initial Spanish experience in America's western territory had not been a good one.

Another group of Spaniards, this one led by explorer Francisco Vásquez de Coronado, also explored the western territories in the 1540s. They mainly sought wealth in the form of gold. Coronado set out from Mexico City early in 1540 and reached what would become the states of Kansas and Colorado a year later. His crew became the first Europeans to find the Continental Divide in the Rocky Mountains. It is the highest elevation point running north to south between the Mississippi River and the Pacific Ocean. This would later become the western boundary of

Hernando de Soto was a Spanish explorer and conquistador who came to North America in search of gold and other riches. His fame was as the explorer who gave Europeans their first look at the American interior. Get the complete story here.

Access this Web site from http://www.myreportlinks.com

the Louisiana Territory. However, Coronado, like de Soto, failed to find prosperous native cities. Coronado returned to Mexico City in 1542.

While the first Spanish explorers did not find what they sought in western America, they had a strong impact on the area and its native population. De Soto especially affected the American Indian civilizations in the area. He brutally attacked the Americans Indians, plundered them of their food supplies, and exposed them to European diseases against which they had no immunity. Many historians consider these to be the major causes of the decline and disappearance of the Mississippian culture. The Mississippians had vanished by the time the next European explorers came to the area.

▶ The French Stake a Claim

Not until 1673 did the Europeans again come to the area around the Mississippi River. In June, a small group of French set out from Canada, then known as New France. They wished to learn about the vast territories to the south and west. This expedition was led by Louis Jolliet and Jacques Marquette. Jolliet was a merchant and mapmaker who was native to North America. Marquette was a missionary who had become familiar with American Indian cultures and customs through years of personal contact.

Like the Spanish, the French hoped to discover a direct water link between the Atlantic and Pacific oceans. They traveled down the Mississippi from the north, near the river's origins. Coming south from what is now Wisconsin, Jolliet and Marquette passed the mouths of the Missouri and Arkansas rivers. They realized that the Mississippi most likely emptied into the Gulf of Mexico to the south. They hoped that the Missouri, whose mouth was wide and discharged into the Mississippi powerfully and turbulently, might

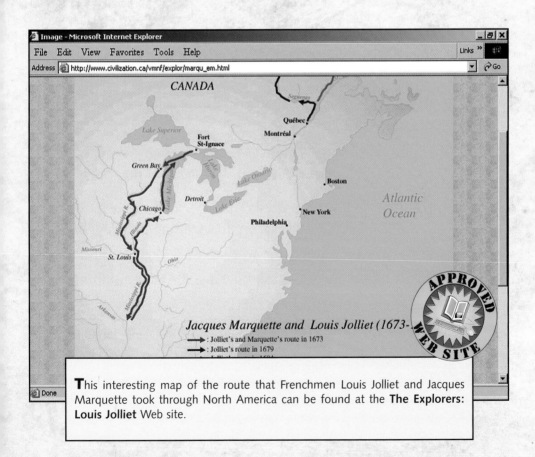

This interesting map of the route that Frenchmen Louis Jolliet and Jacques Marquette took through North America can be found at the **The Explorers: Louis Jolliet** Web site.

provide passage across the western lands to the Pacific.

La Salle's American Adventures

Word spread of the new French discoveries and sparked the interest of a notable explorer and trader, René-Robert Cavelier, Sieur de La Salle. La Salle had extensively explored the area along the southern shores of the Great Lakes that separate the United States from Canada. He became convinced that the river Jolliet and Marquette had explored was the same one found by de Soto and the Spanish. La Salle realized that the nation that controlled the Mississippi River and the surrounding area would control all of North America. He was determined to claim them in the name of France.

In 1677, La Salle was authorized by French King Louis XIV to explore the Mississippi and claim its adjacent lands for France. The king also granted La Salle ownership and trading privileges in the area. Although he wanted to build forts and bases along the Mississippi, La Salle was unable to do so. Nevertheless, La Salle sailed the entire length of the Mississippi in 1682. When he reached the mouth of the river at the Gulf of Mexico, La Salle, with disregard to previous claims by the Spanish, planted a pole and a cross with a French coat of arms at the spot. He claimed

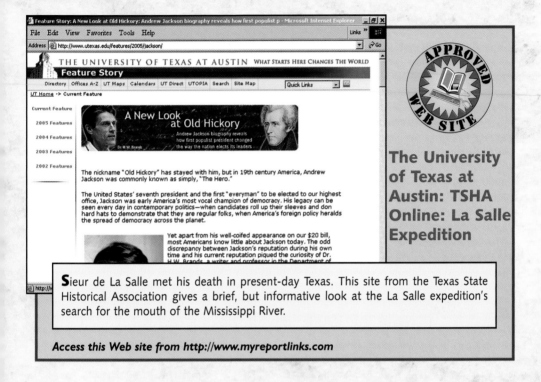

Sieur de La Salle met his death in present-day Texas. This site from the Texas State Historical Association gives a brief, but informative look at the La Salle expedition's search for the mouth of the Mississippi River.

Access this Web site from http://www.myreportlinks.com

the river and all lands that drained into it from the east and west as the property of France. La Salle was the first to name the territory Louisiana, in honor of the French king, and he applied it to the lands both east and west of Mississippi.

The Spanish had let the Louisiana Territory languish after their early explorations. The French did the same thing following the journeys of Jolliet, Marquette, and La Salle. There would not be significant growth and development in Louisiana until the following century.

Unfortunately for La Salle, he never had the opportunity to see French settlement in the areas he explored. La Salle hoped to establish a route for French ships to travel to the land he had claimed. In 1687, he was trying to relocate the river's end from a sea route through the Gulf of Mexico. Instead, he went way off course and landed hundreds of miles to the west, in what is now Texas. La Salle was not a good leader, and a lot of his men did not like him. During the time they were lost, many of the men became ill, some drowned, and they lost one of their ships. In 1687, the men had had enough and killed La Salle.[3]

Iberville, Law, and New Orleans

Early in the 1700s, the efforts of a few people led to new settlements and the establishment of the first major city in the territory, the port city of New Orleans. But even when French people began to travel to, and settle in, the Louisiana Territory, growth and development in the area was marred by trouble.

One person who played a major role in French settlement of Louisiana was a naval officer named Pierre Le Moyne, Sieur d'Iberville. Under his command, a colony of forty-five people was established near the southern end of the Mississippi River. The colony was established mostly to ward off France's colonial rival, Great Britain, who had begun exploration of the western Louisiana Territory. The British were also moving increasingly into the eastern part of the territory, from their

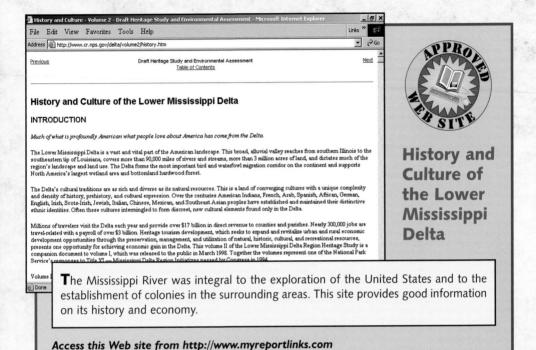

History and Culture - Volume 2 - Draft Heritage Study and Environmental Assessment - Microsoft Internet Explorer

File   Edit   View   Favorites   Tools   Help   Links »

Address http://www.cr.nps.gov/delta/volume2/history.htm   Go

Previous   Draft Heritage Study and Environmental Assessment   Next
                                  Table of Contents

History and Culture of the Lower Mississippi Delta

INTRODUCTION

Much of what is profoundly American what people love about America has come from the Delta.

The Lower Mississippi Delta is a vast and vital part of the American landscape. This broad, alluvial valley reaches from southern Illinois to the southeastern tip of Louisiana, covers more than 90,000 miles of rivers and streams, more than 3 million acres of land, and dictates much of the region's landscape and land use. The Delta forms the most important bird and waterfowl migration corridor on the continent and supports North America's largest wetland area and bottomland hardwood forest.

The Delta's cultural traditions are as rich and diverse as its natural resources. This is a land of converging cultures with a unique complexity and density of history, prehistory, and cultural expression. Over the centuries American Indians, French, Arab, Spanish, African, German, English, Irish, Scots-Irish, Jewish, Italian, Chinese, Mexican, and Southeast Asian peoples have established and maintained their distinctive ethnic identities. Often these cultures intermingled to form discreet, new cultural elements found only in the Delta.

Millions of travelers visit the Delta each year and provide over $17 billion in direct revenue to counties and parishes. Nearly 300,000 jobs are travel-related with a payroll of over $3 billion. Heritage tourism development, which seeks to expand and revitalize urban and rural economic development opportunities through the preservation, management, and utilization of natural, historic, cultural, and recreational resources, presents one opportunity for achieving economic gain in the Delta. This volume II of the Lower Mississippi Delta Region Heritage Study is a companion document to volume I, which was released to the public in March 1998. Together the volumes represent one of the National Park Service's responses to Title XI — Mississippi Delta Region Initiatives passed by Congress in 1994.

History and Culture of the Lower Mississippi Delta

The Mississippi River was integral to the exploration of the United States and to the establishment of colonies in the surrounding areas. This site provides good information on its history and economy.

Access this Web site from http://www.myreportlinks.com

settlements on the East Coast. Yet as much as France wanted to keep Louisiana for themselves and the British out, the French government still did not provide financial support or protection for the new settlers. Iberville's group moved often during the first several years of its existence. Ultimately a colony under the leadership of Iberville's brother, Jean-Baptise, formed the port city of New Orleans. The city had a prime location. The eastern banks of the Mississippi were within a hundred miles of the river's mouth at the Gulf of Mexico. New Orleans quickly grew into a major city. It was designated the capital of Louisiana in 1722, just five years after its founding.

▷ John Law

Elsewhere in the vast Louisiana Territory, brand new settlement was spurred by Scottish financier John Law. He founded the Company of the West to finance and build permanent French settlements. Law did more to promote French development in the Mississippi Valley than any one before him, but his methods were questionable. According to historian Alexander Deconde, "Through shrewd advertising depicting the colony in unrealistically favorable terms, Law aroused interest in Louisiana. Everyone in France with funds to invest, it seemed, wanted to share in the wealth of the colony. . . ."[4] Law's shady land dealings were known as the Mississippi Bubble.

While major settlements never arose north of the Arkansas River, the population in Louisiana grew enormously. The people began to steadily produce crops. Unfortunately, Law built up the population of the territory by bringing people of questionable quality into a very unsettled and unexplored region. He drew heavily from criminal, vagrant, and outcast segments of the French population to increase the number of people living in Louisiana. Law had claimed there were riches to be had from mining and farming in Louisiana. The truth was at the time there were no working mines there and no farms exporting goods outside of the territory. The new French settlements had a

The Library of Congress: France in America

This digital collection incorporates historical documents held by the Library of Congress and the Bibliothèque Nationale de France. Manuscripts, maps, and selections from rare books and journals are included.

Access this Web site from http://www.myreportlinks.com

high failure rate, and many of the new immigrants died of starvation and disease. The great initial success Law had enjoyed was quickly reversed. Investors withdrew their money when the troubled facts about the new Louisiana settlements came to light. There was little growth in the French settlements after the 1720s and little French presence in the area beyond the vicinity of New Orleans.

▶ The French and Indian War

While the French did not show great interest in settling permanently in Louisiana, they continued to venture into the deeper parts of the territory.

Animal furs and hides were still sought after and traded, and the French continued to search for a water passage to the Pacific Ocean. They resented the increasing number of English settlers crossing the Appalachian Mountains and coming into the eastern part of the Louisiana Territory. The English mainly settled along major eastern rivers such as the Ohio, as well as along the shorelines of the Great Lakes. Having laid claim to this land, France grew increasingly hostile to Great Britain during the mid-1700s.

Tensions between the two nations led to the French and Indian War. Unable to match the number of British on the North American continent, the French formed alliances with American Indian

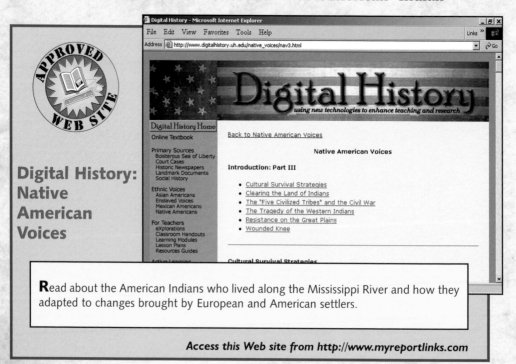

Digital History: Native American Voices

Read about the American Indians who lived along the Mississippi River and how they adapted to changes brought by European and American settlers.

Access this Web site from http://www.myreportlinks.com

△ *Prior to the onset of the French Revolution in 1789, France and the United States were great allies. This is a painting of Frenchman Marquis de Lafayette leading American soldiers at the Battle of Yorktown.*

tribes to fight them. They also built extensive fortifications throughout the territory, just as La Salle had wanted to do nearly a hundred years earlier. The British had stronger naval forces as well as more people in America. They were able to defeat the French and Indians over the course of this nine-year war. (The war also spread to Europe and was part of a larger conflict known as the Seven Years' War). In February 1763, an agreement known as the Treaty of Paris between Great Britain and France gave Britain control of the eastern part of the Louisiana Territory. The western part of the territory, and the small area from New Orleans to the Gulf of Mexico along the Mississippi's eastern shore, were ceded to Spain. At this point only the area under Spanish control—New Orleans and the land west of the Mississippi—was referred to as the Louisiana Territory. The eastern sections became part of the British colonies in America.

▶ Revolutionary War

Control of the eastern sections changed hands once again following the Revolutionary War. The British turned the territory over to the United States when the thirteen original colonies won their independence in 1783. What had once been eastern Louisiana was now part of the United States. Western Louisiana was still under Spanish control. Challenges over the status of the remaining Louisiana Territory quickly led to turmoil.

WRANGLING OVER SPANISH LOUISIANA

Early on, many people believed the United States was destined to possess all of the land of central North America. Its borders would stretch from the Atlantic to the Pacific coasts. Some even believed that the United States would and should also take over the land that is now Canada and other lands in Mexico and Central America. This belief was called Manifest Destiny. Exploration and settlement by colonists in the eastern territories, now referred to as the American West or American Frontier, had been occurring since well before the United States officially took control there. Western Louisiana also became increasingly influenced by American settlement and trade in the years after independence. Yet the major European powers had a continued interest in the Louisiana Territory. The area became a flash point for conflict and intrigue among the four nations— France, Spain, Great Britain, and the United States—that wanted access to the region.

A Tide of Western Expansion

The westward expansion of American settlers during the late eighteenth century was enormous. Populations increased fourfold in the territories of Kentucky and Tennessee, which became states during the 1790s. Population growth among Americans was not as great in Spanish-held Louisiana, but there was significant migration of Americans. The Americans were settling west of the Mississippi River and into the region along the eastern shore at the mouth of the river, which included New Orleans. Some Americans became prominent and powerful in Spanish territory. They

This is a lithograph created by George A. Crofutt based on a painting called "America in Progress" by John Gast. In the painting, it shows Americans fulfilling their Manifest Destiny by settling the West.

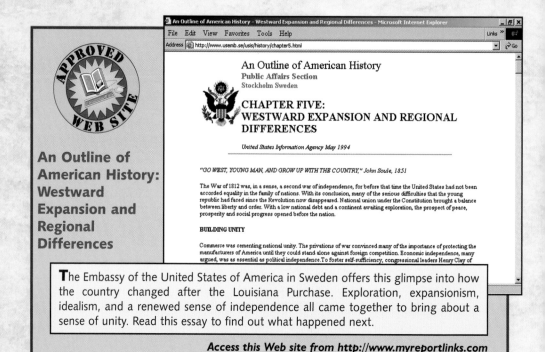

An Outline of
American History:
Westward
Expansion and
Regional
Differences

An Outline of American History
Public Affairs Section
Stockholm Sweden

CHAPTER FIVE:
WESTWARD EXPANSION AND REGIONAL DIFFERENCES

United States Information Agency May 1994

"GO WEST, YOUNG MAN, AND GROW UP WITH THE COUNTRY," John Soule, 1851

The War of 1812 was, in a sense, a second war of independence, for before that time the United States had not been accorded equality in the family of nations. With its conclusion, many of the serious difficulties that the young republic had faced since the Revolution now disappeared. National union under the Constitution brought a balance between liberty and order. With a low national debt and a continent awaiting exploration, the prospect of peace, prosperity and social progress opened before the nation.

BUILDING UNITY

Commerce was cementing national unity. The privations of war convinced many of the importance of protecting the manufacturers of America until they could stand alone against foreign competition. Economic independence, many argued, was as essential as political independence. To foster self-sufficiency, congressional leaders Henry Clay of

The Embassy of the United States of America in Sweden offers this glimpse into how the country changed after the Louisiana Purchase. Exploration, expansionism, idealism, and a renewed sense of independence all came together to bring about a sense of unity. Read this essay to find out what happened next.

Access this Web site from http://www.myreportlinks.com

controlled some town governments and were leading landholders and businesspeople in many places in Louisiana.

Perhaps American power was most evident in trade. With its major urban and coastal areas close by, the United States utilized the western territory in ways that European nations had not. The vast land produced a wealth of farming and forestry products that could be sold. Spain controlled shipping in New Orleans, but the productivity of the region was dependent on Americans.

Most trade moved through the vast river system that led to the Mississippi. It was easier to transport goods thousands of miles by river and sea to the East Coast, than to haul goods hundreds of miles over the Appalachian Mountains. The success and even survival of the western American settlers depended heavily on access to the Mississippi River.

Spanish-American Tension

Spain looked down on the movement of Americans into Spanish-held territory. It regarded the territory as a buffer zone for Spanish territories in the South and West that were sources for mining and mineral wealth. Spain could not afford to place large military forces in Louisiana. Spanish leaders encouraged and financed American Indian attacks against settlers from the East, just as the French had done. Some of these American Indian attacks were ferocious. Alexander McGillivray was a warrior from the Creek Nation who was also part Scottish. He led a particularly damaging war against American settlers in the South in the 1780s. However, rapid growth of American settlements in the western frontier continued.

Another hostile act by the Spanish government was the closing of the lower Mississippi River and the port of New Orleans to all foreigners in 1784. This stirred great anger among western Americans. It intensified their desire for the United States to take control of the Louisiana

The Mississippi River flowing through Arkansas.

Territory and the rest of the western territory. The decree was also unpopular among the Spanish in North America. Merchants and seafarers depended heavily on trade in American goods, and most Spanish people in North America had come to rely on food produced by American farmers. To protect their own interest, the Spanish in Louisiana largely disregarded the prohibitions against foreign trade when it came to Americans. The Spanish government's measures were not effective in deterring Americans from moving to or doing business in Louisiana. Instead, they incited anti-Spanish feelings among Americans. They also gave rise to greater demands on the United States government from its people to gain control of the Mississippi River at the very least.

▷ Encouraging Treason

Spain also encouraged western Americans to break with the United States and form a new nation or become a Spanish colony. The Spanish had always required Americans settling in Louisiana to declare loyalty to the Spanish crown. Few Americans took this oath seriously. With increasing numbers of people moving into the vast, open areas in the north of the territory, it became impossible for the Spanish to enforce. Spain offered to guarantee complete access to the lower Mississippi to any people living in a territory that broke from the United States and agreed to become Spanish citizens. This was known as the Spanish Conspiracy. Like other attempts by Spain to prevent the spread of Americans westward, this one also failed.

After three years, Spain agreed to allow Americans to trade and transport goods through New Orleans. At first Americans were required to pay a 15 percent tax on these goods, but in 1795, Spain and the United States reached an agreement. The Treaty of San Lorenzo removed the tax from American goods in New Orleans, gave

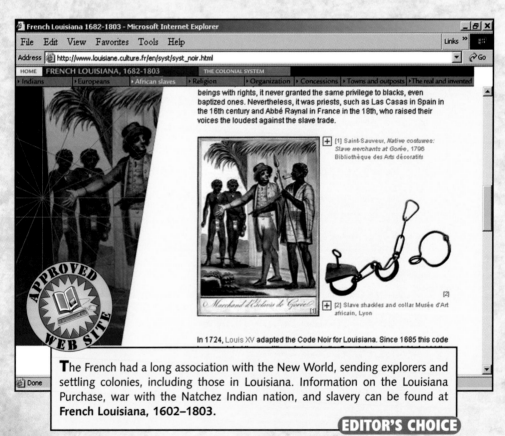

The French had a long association with the New World, sending explorers and settling colonies, including those in Louisiana. Information on the Louisiana Purchase, war with the Natchez Indian nation, and slavery can be found at **French Louisiana, 1602–1803.**

EDITOR'S CHOICE

Americans full navigational rights through the Mississippi River, and committed the Spanish to stop inciting American Indian attacks against American frontier dwellers. Spain did not agree to these terms indefinitely, but guaranteed Americans an ongoing right to trade without being taxed, either through New Orleans or other southern Mississippi ports.

This agreement did not eliminate tensions between Spain and the United States, but it did ease them. Within a few years, though, international developments threw Louisiana into chaos once again.

Rumors of a French Return

While most Americans wanted to take control of the entire western territory, many were willing to accept the Spanish presence there. Although Spain had once been a formidable world power, its influence in the world had long been in decline. Spain was not viewed as a military threat to the United States. It was widely believed that Spain would eventually turn Louisiana over to the United States, rather than continue to pay the cost of maintaining the colony.[1]

Like Spain, France had also seen its power decline during the eighteenth century. The loss to the British in the French and Indian War had been just one example of defeat suffered by France in combat over its overseas colonies. Furthermore, a revolution in France in 1789 had left the nation in turmoil. Then, late in the 1790s, great change came to France. The nation once again emerged as a major power, dominant in continental Europe. There would also be a revived interest in pursuing an international empire.

France's renewed interest in foreign colonialism, combined with Spain's sense of being burdened by the Louisiana Territory, led to the Treaty of San Ildefonso. The treaty was named after the Spanish city where it was signed. The governments of both countries intended to keep the agreement secret, but rumors and reports of it spread quickly. Although they were unconfirmed and even denied by France and Spain, reports about the treaty caused an uproar in the United States, especially among the western settlers.

▶ Napoléon and Jefferson

The resurgence of French strength had been almost entirely due to the emergence of Napoléon Bonaparte as a military conqueror and national leader. Napoléon is widely recognized as one of the most important figures in world history. Few other leaders transformed a nation so much in a short time as did Napoléon. Using a combination of military prowess, cunning, personal charisma, and ruthlessness, Napoléon seized power in 1799 and quickly imposed his rule. Without Napoléon's drive and powerful leadership, France probably would not have had a renewed interest in Louisiana. For Napoléon though, maintaining colonies was a natural next step to conquests France had made during a series of wars against its European neighbors.

Another formidable leader came to power in the United States. Thomas Jefferson became the third United States president just as unofficial reports about the San Ildefonso Treaty reached the United States. Jefferson, the author of the Declaration of Independence, had been a high-ranking member of the government since the birth of the nation. He was an expert on foreign affairs, and had served as President Washington's secretary of state. In that role, he dealt with France quite a bit. Not as ruthless as Napoléon, Jefferson was cunning and sharp.

▷ Mounting French-American Tensions

Jefferson assumed the presidency with positive feelings toward France. He had been United States minister to that country following the Revolutionary War. A student and admirer of French society and culture, he was appreciative of the help France had given the United States during the Revolutionary War. Not all Americans felt the same way. Many were dismayed at the violence

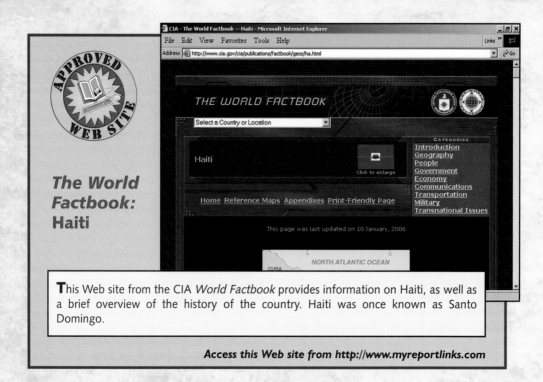

The World Factbook: Haiti

THE WORLD FACTBOOK

Select a Country or Location

Haiti

Click to enlarge

CATEGORIES
Introduction
Geography
People
Government
Economy
Communications
Transportation
Military
Transnational Issues

Home Reference Maps Appendixes Print-Friendly Page

This page was last updated on 10 January, 2006

NORTH ATLANTIC OCEAN

CUBA

This Web site from the CIA *World Factbook* provides information on Haiti, as well as a brief overview of the history of the country. Haiti was once known as Santo Domingo.

Access this Web site from http://www.myreportlinks.com

and chaos in France during the French Revolution of 1789 to 1799. They regarded France as a far different country from the one that had aided the United States against Great Britain. Americans resented damage caused to American overseas trade during the wars between France and other European nations. Many Americans were uncertain about Jefferson and his pro-French feelings.

These feelings were intensified when, shortly after becoming president, Jefferson pledged support for an agreement called the Treaty of Mortefontaine. In it, the United States pledged support for France in its effort to retake a rebellious colony in the Caribbean Sea. Santo Domingo on the island of Hispaniola is now the location of Haiti and the Dominican Republic. Santo Domingo been one of France's most productive colonies. Large amounts of coffee, sugar, cocoa, and other crops were grown there. Production was dependent on a slave population that was much larger than the free population.

▷ Slave Revolt

In 1791 the slaves revolted and took control of the island. Santo Domingo was then ruled by former slave and rebel leader Toussaint-L'Ouverture. Americans who opposed France considered L'Ouverture an ally. The previous American president, John Adams, had supported him to prevent England from capturing the island. For these Americans, Jefferson's reversal of policy against L'Ouverture was treachery.

Jefferson's popularity in the West was hurt again when the news about the Treaty of Mortefontaine became known in the United States. It set off a widespread anti-French backlash. His political opponents used Jefferson's support of the French against him to try put pressure on him to be aggressive in dealing with France over Louisiana and New Orleans.

Jefferson, however, was determined not to allow France to resume control of New Orleans. Secretary of State James Madison conveyed to

Louis Andre Pichon, French diplomat to the United States, how severe the reaction would be to a French takeover of New Orleans. As historian Thomas Fleming recounts, "Madison summoned Pichon to his office and told him in the grimmest tones that France's plans were propelling both countries into a disastrous war. In no-nonsense phrases, the secretary of state warned the French diplomat that the Americans insisted on obtaining New Orleans. . . ."[2]

▶ Growing French Boldness

The Treaty of Mortefontaine also led to potential trouble for Jefferson across the Atlantic Ocean. While Jefferson may have viewed the treaty with

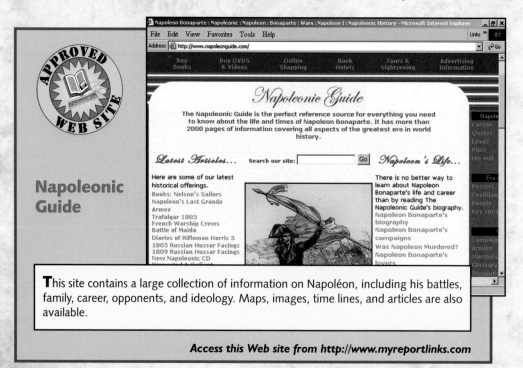

Napoleonic Guide

This site contains a large collection of information on Napoléon, including his battles, family, career, opponents, and ideology. Maps, images, time lines, and articles are also available.

Access this Web site from http://www.myreportlinks.com

France as a measure of cooperation between
the two countries, many viewed it differently in
France. Before they knew how strongly Jefferson
opposed the French returning to Louisiana,
Napoléon and his deputies regarded the agreement
as a sign of American weakness. They thought the
United States was not going to challenge a strong
French presence in North America. This treaty with
the United States came just a day before the treaty
with Spain that returned the Louisiana Territory
and New Orleans to France.

Confident that France could suppress opposition in Santo Domingo, Napoléon assembled a
large military force to dispatch to the island. Once
the French troops controlled the island, they
would occupy the Louisiana Territory. A force of
twenty thousand troops sailed from France to
America in the fall of 1801. It was commanded by
Napoléon's brother-in-law, General Charles Leclerc.
Napoléon was certain Leclerc would succeed.[3]

Napoléon's assuredness about quick and easy
victory in Santo Domingo proved premature. In
fact, the venture became so costly and damaging
to France that it changed Napoléon's plans regarding North America.

MAKING THE DEAL: FRANCE AND AMERICA

LOUISIANA PURCHASE

As 1802 began, it appeared that a war with France over Louisiana and New Orleans was a possibility. The leaders of both countries had shown a strong willingness to fight over the New Orleans region. There was lingering resentment over the conflict that had occurred between the two countries during the war of the previous decade between Britain and France when France was intercepting American shipping. The unofficial news about the transfer of Louisiana and New Orleans had set off heated feelings on the part of both the French and Americans. Yet the situation was ultimately settled peacefully. This was partly because of severe losses suffered by France in its attempt to reassert control in Santo Domingo, which left far less troops and resources for protecting the territories. Other unexpected problems discouraged Napoléon from pursuing his plans in North America.

▷ Setbacks in Santo Domingo

The attempt to retake Santo Domingo from L'Ouverture's army turned out to be difficult. After arriving in January 1802, Leclerc's forces captured the coastal cities and the part of the island that had once belonged to Spain. The rural areas remained under the control of the rebels. An assault by the rebels in February almost resulted in total defeat for the French. The boldness and bravery of General Jean Baptiste Donatien de Rochambeau gave France the advantage over L'Ouverture. In May, the rebel leader agreed to negotiate a treaty that turned power over to the French but allowed him to remain on the island on his own property. The French later broke the agreement by abducting L'Ouverture and shipping him to France. He was imprisoned in a remote area and died a year later.[1]

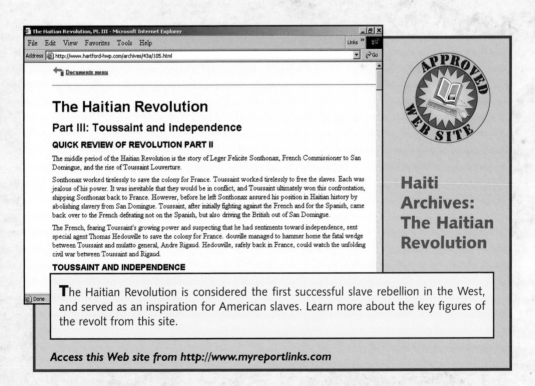

Haiti Archives: The Haitian Revolution

The Haitian Revolution is considered the first successful slave rebellion in the West, and served as an inspiration for American slaves. Learn more about the key figures of the revolt from this site.

Access this Web site from http://www.myreportlinks.com

For a while, the French managed to subdue the rebellion through continued force, bribes to rebel leaders, and by claiming that they would not reinstate slavery on the island.

Meanwhile, the French forces continued to suffer setbacks on Santo Domingo. Relying on the Treaty of Mortefontaine, the French expected assistance from the Americans. Instead, anti-French sentiment had increased since the time that treaty had been signed. American merchants in the Caribbean Sea refused to supply provisions to the French without demanding exceedingly high prices. The American government was not willing to loan money to the French or otherwise assist in the attack against the rebels. American leaders were growing suspicious that the huge fighting force sent by Napoléon was not just there to subdue Santo Domingo. They correctly figured that some of the contingent was intended to solidify Louisiana. There was also some support for L'Ouverture in the United States. Many Americans opposed slavery and others simply thought it was to the United States' advantage to have him disrupt the American colonies of France or any European nation.

▷ Yellow Fever

Probably the biggest problem facing the French forces in Santo Domingo was disease. France had incurred serious losses during the height of combat.

In addition, French troops continued to die by the thousands when the tropical disease known as yellow fever broke out among them. At that time, yellow fever had a fatality rate of about 85 percent. By the summer of 1802, it had so ravaged the French forces that only about four thousand, one fifth the original number, remained. With the French Army so badly weakened, rebels staged renewed attacks when it was learned that France planned to reinstate slavery on the island. The renewed fighting reduced French forces even further. Leclerc died of yellow fever in November of that year. The remaining French forces in Santo Domingo were not capable of sailing on to Louisiana and effectively claiming and defending it.

A Chorus of Calls for War

In the United States, western settlers felt that the leaders in the East did not care about them. Their concerns were heightened by the threat of a French takeover in Louisiana. There was talk of secession by the western territories. Some Americans called for an immediate attack against New Orleans and Louisiana to take both territories before the French had time to deliver troops there. As far back as December 1801, "Federalists clamored almost automatically for the forceable seizure of the city."[2] Jefferson's political opponents also used the situation to try to turn public opinion in the country against him and his political party, the Democratic Republicans. The opposing Federalist party was led by Alexander Hamilton, Jefferson's longtime political foe. Hamilton was a former aide to General Washington during the Revolutionary War. He later served as secretary of the treasury under Washington. Those favoring an immediate invasion of the Spanish-held territories in North America before the French arrived viewed Hamilton as a compelling leader for the conquest.

Strong pro-war sentiment in the United States intensified even further when the Spanish had reimposed trade restrictions on Americans in

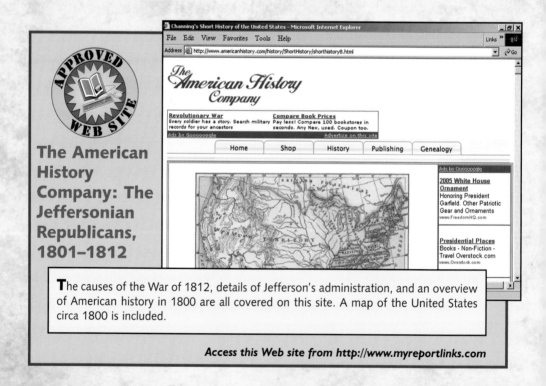

The American History Company: The Jeffersonian Republicans, 1801–1812

The causes of the War of 1812, details of Jefferson's administration, and an overview of American history in 1800 are all covered on this site. A map of the United States circa 1800 is included.

Access this Web site from http://www.myreportlinks.com

New Orleans in October 1802. This raised war sentiment among the public to a fever pitch, especially in the West. Many Americans were convinced that France and Spain had schemed together to reimpose trade restrictions as a prelude to occupying the territory. The French could then claim that they were just continuing the existing trade policies in effect in New Orleans.

Jefferson and other United States government officials protested the new trade restrictions vigorously and pressured the national Spanish government. Spain lifted the restrictions the following March, but in the meantime, Jefferson's political opponents became even more fierce in their criticism. The combination of rising public fury over a potential French invasion of Louisiana and New Orleans, and the scathing attacks launched against Jefferson by Federalist leaders, put his presidency and even the United States government into a potential crisis situation.

Turning to James Monroe

Jefferson was looking to make a stronger statement regarding the United States government's commitment to at least assure its people access to the Mississippi River. He appointed James Monroe to be a special envoy to France. Monroe joined Livingston in Paris, but dealt specifically with resolving the issues of the Louisiana Territory and

A portrait of James Monroe created between 1830 and 1842 by D. W. Kellogg.

New Orleans, and control of the Mississippi River. Monroe was a longtime friend and political associate of Jefferson's, and he also owned land and did business in the western territories. Monroe was highly regarded among frontier people. With Monroe's appointment, Jefferson hoped to convey to both the French and Americans that he was treating the situation surrounding Louisiana with the utmost importance.

Pressure on Jefferson

The Federalists continued to criticize Jefferson and portray him as weak and ineffective against Napoléon. A series of speeches by Federalists in the United States Senate claimed that Jefferson was being too passive. They felt that instead of appointing Monroe to negotiate with France, the United States should immediately take military action. One senator, Gouverneur Morris of New York, challenged Jefferson's Republican Democratic followers in the Senate regarding their approach to dealing with Napoléon: "He wants power; You have no power. He wants dominion; you have no dominion . . . that you can grant. He wants influence in Europe, and have you any influence in Europe? What in the name of heaven are the means by which you would render this negotiation succesful?"[3] Newspapers and publications that favored Federalists expressed glowing support for speeches like these and relentlessly targeted Jefferson and the Democrats for their alleged softness. Alexander Hamilton owned a New York newspaper, the *New York Evening Post,* in which he wrote such pieces. He used a false name to make it seem like the articles were written by someone not directly involved in government.

Indeed, as Monroe embarked for France in early 1803, it appeared that Napoléon might be unable to be talked out of waging war. The French leader appointed to preside over Louisiana and New Orleans, Pierre Clement de Laussat, had already set sail for North America. In spite of the

This map of the Mississippi River shows how the region was marked around the time of the Louisiana Purchase.

massive losses suffered by the French in Santo Domingo, another large military contingent consisting of three thousand troops had been assembled in Helvoet Sluys, a harbor in French-occupied territory in Holland. There was little doubt among Americans that it could only be intended as an occupying force in Louisiana. All the while,

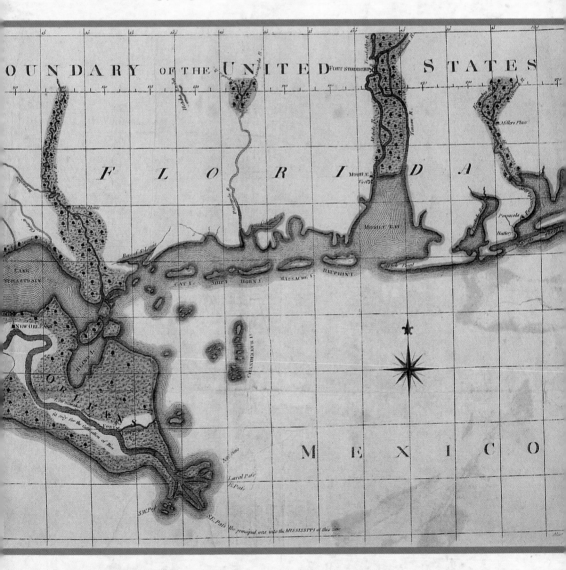

Charles-Maurice de Talleyrand-Périgord had been resisting American diplomat Robert Livingston's attempts to make a deal with the French that would lead to a peaceful resolution over the Louisiana Territory and New Orleans.

▶ The Livingston-Talleyrand Negotiations

Talleyrand had a long history of deviousness and cunning. In dealing with Livingston, Talleyrand continued the same kind of behavior. He looked to get as much out of the situation as possible for himself as well as France. While Napoléon seemed intent on taking the North American territories, Talleyrand tried to obtain the greatest possible

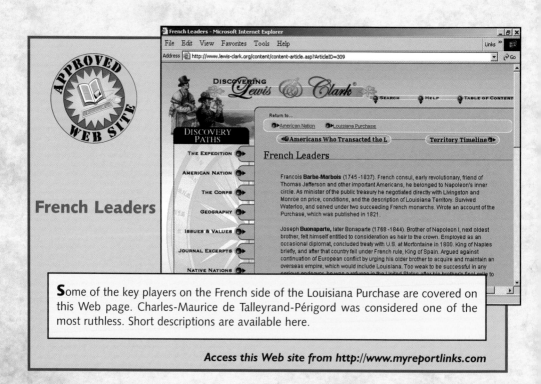

Some of the key players on the French side of the Louisiana Purchase are covered on this Web page. Charles-Maurice de Talleyrand-Périgord was considered one of the most ruthless. Short descriptions are available here.

Access this Web site from http://www.myreportlinks.com

concessions from Livingston without ever actually claiming that Louisiana or New Orleans might be offered by France. Indeed, Talleyrand continued to insist almost throughout the negotiation that the territories had not even been turned over to France by Spain.

After Napoléon changed his mind and decided to sell Louisiana and New Orleans to the United States, Talleyrand also tried to work that to his advantage. He subtly indicated that Napoléon might be willing to make a deal for Louisiana and New Orleans before Napoléon had revealed it. By doing so, Talleyrand bolstered his bargaining position and hoped to profit from it. If he could get a higher price for the territories than Napoléon had originally set, Talleyrand might quietly be granted some of the additional money. Once negotiations with the United States were passed into the hands of Francois Barbé-Marbois, Talleyrand joined the ranks of officials trying to break them up.

Talleyrand's Tactics

Having lost the chance to benefit from the Louisiana deal, Talleyrand attempted to obtain a peace agreement with Great Britain that would sway Napoléon not to pursue another war with that country. Napoléon had been planning for war with Great Britain. This was a big reason he had for abandoning plans to possess and occupy

Louisiana and New Orleans. He would need the money and troops to fight the British.

Talleyrand and other French leaders now opposed to the Louisiana Purchase hoped that a treaty with Britain would stop the sale because the money would no longer be needed. It is not hard to understand why, when confronted with the possibility of having to resume talking with Talleyrand, Livingston and Monroe decided to settle the transaction quickly with Barbé-Marbois.

▷ Napoléon's Shift

Certainly the threat of war with Great Britain weighed heavily in Napoléon's decision to sell both New Orleans and Louisiana to the United States. Neither the threat of war with the United States nor the thrashing of his forces in Santo Domingo had been enough to convince him to give up on the North American territories. The cost of a major war with France's most powerful regional foe was just too much for the nation to sustain. Furthermore, the forces Napoléon had gathered in Holland had been blocked by frozen harbor conditions during the winter and a British blockade in the spring.

In deciding to sell Louisiana and New Orleans, Napoléon did not give up hopes of taking power in western America in the long term. However, for the present, he needed to focus his nation's full

A painting of Charles-Maurice de Talleyrand-Périgord by artist Ary Scheffer.

attention and resources on yet another military conflict with Great Britain.

Barbé-Marbois Makes the Deal

When Napoléon assigned Barbé-Marbois to handle the negotiations with the Americans on the disputed territories, he said he wanted at least 50 million francs, about $12.5 million at that time. Barbé-Marbois originally asked for twice that amount, and ended up receiving 60 million francs, about $15 million, from the Americans. That was more than Napoléon had demanded as a minimum, and the Americans also agreed to cover costs of American merchants' claims against France, bringing the total cost to $20 million.

Barbé-Marbois benefited from a stronger negotiating position than either of the Americans involved. Unlike Monroe or Livingston, Barbé-Marbois knew that there was internal disagreement within the French government concerning the sale of Louisiana and New Orleans. He understood that delay could mean the withdrawal of the treaty offer. Barbé-Marbois also had the benefit of easy access to his own government. Early nineteenth-century communication and transportation prevented the American representatives from having this. It took weeks to send a message overseas to Washington.

Indeed, Livingston and Monroe had to conclude a settlement without ever officially receiving

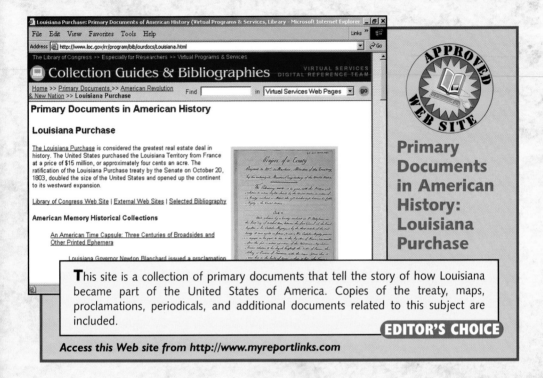

Primary Documents in American History: Louisiana Purchase

This site is a collection of primary documents that tell the story of how Louisiana became part of the United States of America. Copies of the treaty, maps, proclamations, periodicals, and additional documents related to this subject are included.

EDITOR'S CHOICE

Access this Web site from http://www.myreportlinks.com

permission to purchase the entire Louisiana Territory. They had only been told to try to obtain New Orleans (and because of the false belief that Florida was also coming into French possession, that territory as well). The fact is that Secretary of State Madison authorized the purchase of all of Louisiana and New Orleans as soon as he received word that the French had raised that possibility. But the American negotiators would not receive that message by the time Barbé-Marbois issued his final offer, at which point the Americans felt they had to act.

On May 2, 1803, three weeks after the first late-night meeting between Robert Livingston and

Barbé-Marbois, the Louisiana Purchase agreement was reached between French and American negotiators. The final deal was sealed in Barbé-Marbois's finance minister's office. Napoléon gave final French approval on May 22. The potentially explosive situation surrounding the western American territories had been resolved, and there would not be war between France and the United States. However, there was still much to be done and obstacles to overcome before the territories could actually be transferred into the United States' possession. In fact, the territories of Louisiana and New Orleans would not be fully and securely under United States control for several more years.

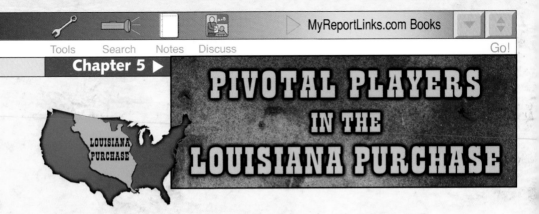

PIVOTAL PLAYERS IN THE LOUISIANA PURCHASE

While many people contributed to the Louisiana Purchase, only a few played a critical role. Because the uprising in Santo Domingo proved to be so costly and damaging to French forces, Toussaint-L'Ouverture could be said to have made a significant difference in bringing about the agreement.

As United States president, Thomas Jefferson exhibited a determination to secure access to the Mississippi River and the vital port of New Orleans for western Americans. He also showed restraint in the face of criticism and a willingness to settle the conflict with France through negotiations.

Among the people involved in the Louisiana Purchase, though, clearly Napoléon was the most important player. The decision not to try to defend Louisiana and New Orleans and turn them over to the United States for cash payment was solely Napoléon's. Although it may have been costly for him to have tried to take and hold possession of the territories, he had a strong enough military to

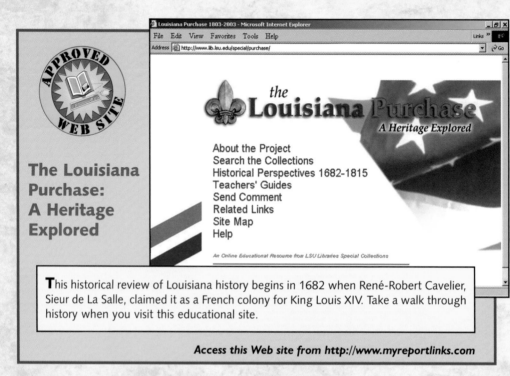

The Louisiana Purchase: A Heritage Explored

Louisiana Purchase 1803-2003 - Microsoft Internet Explorer

File   Edit   View   Favorites   Tools   Help   Links »

Address http://www.lib.lsu.edu/special/purchase/   Go

the **Louisiana Purchase**
A Heritage Explored

About the Project
Search the Collections
Historical Perspectives 1682-1815
Teachers' Guides
Send Comment
Related Links
Site Map
Help

An Online Educational Resource from LSU Libraries Special Collections

This historical review of Louisiana history begins in 1682 when René-Robert Cavelier, Sieur de La Salle, claimed it as a French colony for King Louis XIV. Take a walk through history when you visit this educational site.

Access this Web site from http://www.myreportlinks.com

make the effort. Plus, most of the French people and many French government officials opposed giving up Louisiana and New Orleans. So, it is unlikely that, had anyone else but Napoléon been in control of France, the decision to sell those territories would yet have been made. Historian and author Michael Hart summed up Napoléon's overriding importance in bringing about the Louisiana Purchase:

> Napoléon . . . was not solely responsible for the Louisiana Purchase. The American Government clearly played a role as well. But the French offer was such a bargain it seems likely that any American government would have accepted it, while the decision to sell the Louisiana Territory

came about through the arbitrary judgement of a single individual, Napoléon Bonaparte.[1]

Napoléon Bonaparte: A Legend of World History

Napoléon Bonaparte is considered one of the most important military and government leaders in world history. He achieved stunning success on the battlefield, gained a large and enthusiastic following in France, and seized and held power in that country for many years during an unstable period. He credibly claimed to be emperor over much of Europe during a time when France was at the height of its national power. In addition, Napoléon introduced new forms and methods of civil and government administration and legal codes that have since been adapted and followed by many nations. Even with all this, allowing the Louisiana Purchase is considered one of the most important and influential actions Napoléon ever made. It aided the development and emergence of the United States as a major world nation.

As much as he is associated with French nationalism, Napoléon was not of French origin. Indeed, in his early years Napoléon was passionately anti-French. He was born on the Mediterranean island of Corsica on August 15, 1769, which had only become a French possession the year before. His wealthy parents were of noble

Napoléon seated at his home, Fontainebleau.

Italian heritage. Anti-French sentiment ran strong among the members of the household, yet Napoléon was enrolled by his father in a French military academy at age nine.

Early Adult Years

Napoléon proved to be an excellent student at the first military academy he attended. He was recruited by the leading military academy in Paris, where he enrolled in 1784. Just one year later, at age sixteen, he joined the French Army as a second lieutenant. When the French Revolution broke out in 1789, Napoléon joined a group called the Jacobins that favored a democratic form of government for France. This group rose to power just as Napoléon was climbing the ranks of the military. By mid-1793, Napoléon had risen to the rank of captain in the army, while the Jacobins had taken control of the French government.

Napoléon quickly made his name as a great military commander. He defeated the British at the Battle of Toulon in late 1793. Napoléon was then made a general, and enjoyed continued success against Italian armies and the powerful Austrian Army. Under his leadership, France became the major power in continental Europe. In November 1799, he led a revolt against the government in control of France, which consisted of elected legislative bodies and an enforcement branch known as the Directory. Napoléon then installed a new form of government, a three level directory in which only one person, Napoléon himself, wielded any actual power.

Building An Empire

Following this, Napoléon continued his success in conquering territory on the European continent. By 1810, Napoléon controlled a major part of Europe ranging from Holland in the west, Poland in the east, and Northern Italy in the south. Although he had originally risen to power by opposing France's royal system and supporting the causes of common people, as a ruler Napoléon

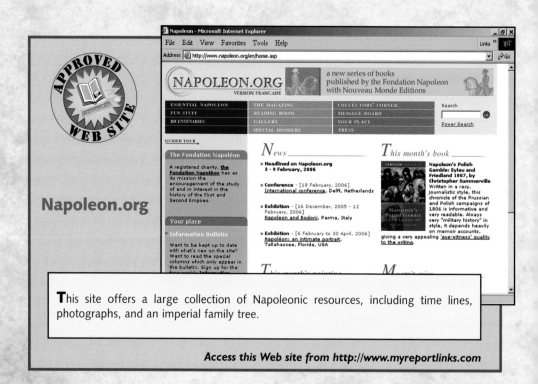

Napoleon.org

This site offers a large collection of Napoleonic resources, including time lines, photographs, and an imperial family tree.

Access this Web site from http://www.myreportlinks.com

exhibited the same behavior as the former royal leaders. He had himself crowned emperor and his wife, Josephine, crowned empress.

▶ Napoleonic Code

In spite of this, Napoléon advanced the rights of peasants and middle class citizens during his reign. The legal and civil code he implemented, which came to be known as the Napoleonic Code, gave equal legal rights to all people regardless of wealth or family status. The code was practiced in French-held areas while Napoléon ruled, and was also later adapted by many other nations. Along with the decision to allow for the Louisiana Purchase, the creation of the Napoleonic Code is regarded as one of Napoléon's greatest lasting historic contributions.

Napoléon's fortunes began to change in 1812. In June of that year, his armies invaded Russia. Initially he was highly successful, reaching the Russian capital of Moscow and occupying it in October. However, Napoléon's forces eventually had to retreat. In the meantime, Napoléon had left Paris undefended. During his absence the allied armies invaded the city, which surrendered with little struggle. By this time Napoléon had lost the support of the leading officers in the French military. On his return to Paris, Napoléon abdicated as French ruler.

▶ Napoléon's Demise

The nations allied against France restored its banished monarchy and exiled Napoléon to a small Mediterranean island called Elba. However, Napoléon anticipated that the new government would prove unpopular in France and that he would have the opportunity to return to power. In February 1815, Napoléon concluded the time was ripe. He escaped from his forced exile and landed on the French mainland with about a thousand followers. He gained additional recruits as he marched toward Paris, and because the French Army once again aligned themselves with Napoléon, he was able to drive out the restored

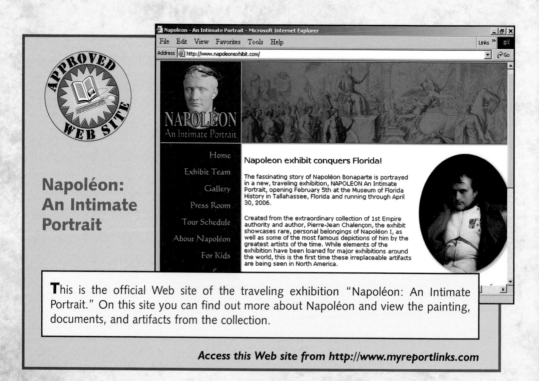

Napoléon: An Intimate Portrait

Napoleon exhibit conquers Florida!

The fascinating story of Napoléon Bonaparte is portrayed in a new, traveling exhibition, NAPOLEON An Intimate Portrait, opening February 5th at the Museum of Florida History in Tallahassee, Florida and running through April 30, 2006.

Created from the extraordinary collection of 1st Empire authority and author, Pierre-Jean Chalençon, the exhibit showcases rare, personal belongings of Napoléon I, as well as some of the most famous depictions of him by the greatest artists of the time. While elements of the exhibition have been loaned for major exhibitions around the world, this is the first time these irreplaceable artifacts are being seen in North America.

This is the official Web site of the traveling exhibition "Napoléon: An Intimate Portrait." On this site you can find out more about Napoléon and view the painting, documents, and artifacts from the collection.

Access this Web site from http://www.myreportlinks.com

monarch rulers in March. However, his second reign was short-lived. The nations that had previously allied themselves against Napoléon reacted immediately, and Napoléon's army was defeated at the decisive Battle of Waterloo in June 1815. Once again, Napoléon was exiled, this time to the distant South Atlantic island of St. Helena. He remained there until his death in 1821.

▷ Thomas Jefferson: A National Hero

Thomas Jefferson is one of the people commonly referred to as the Founding Fathers of the United States. Along with such notables as George Washington, John Adams, and Benjamin Franklin, Jefferson played a major role in leading the American Revolution against Great Britain in the 1770s. He is also one of four presidents commemorated on Mount Rushmore. It was as United States president that Jefferson played an instrumental role in the Louisiana Purchase through his commitment to American expansion. In a letter to James Monroe in 1801 Jefferson wrote, "It is impossible not to look forward to distant times, when our rapid multiplication will expand itself beyond those limits, and cover the whole northern, if not the southern continent . . ."[2]

Jefferson was born in Shadwell, Virginia, in 1743. His father, Peter Jefferson, had enjoyed success as both a land surveyor and a crop planter.

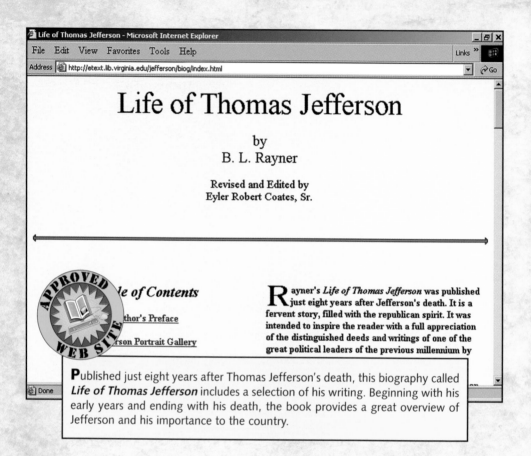

Life of Thomas Jefferson - Microsoft Internet Explorer

File   Edit   View   Favorites   Tools   Help   Links »

Address http://etext.lib.virginia.edu/jefferson/biog/index.html   Go

Life of Thomas Jefferson

by
B. L. Rayner

Revised and Edited by
Eyler Robert Coates, Sr.

le of Contents

thor's Preface

rson Portrait Gallery

Rayner's *Life of Thomas Jefferson* was published
just eight years after Jefferson's death. It is a
fervent story, filled with the republican spirit. It was
intended to inspire the reader with a full appreciation
of the distinguished deeds and writings of one of the
great political leaders of the previous millennium by

Done

Published just eight years after Thomas Jefferson's death, this biography called
Life of Thomas Jefferson includes a selection of his writing. Beginning with his
early years and ending with his death, the book provides a great overview of
Jefferson and his importance to the country.

His mother, Jane Randolph, came from a wealthy
family. Jefferson, like Napoléon, enjoyed privilege
and comfort in his early years.

Jefferson attended the College of William and
Mary for two years, but never received a degree.
He studied law and became a lawyer at age twenty-
three. In addition to practicing law, Jefferson also
continued his father's crop-planting operation at
Monticello, the family estate he had inherited
while still in his teens. Although he was in favor of
stopping the spread of slavery, Jefferson came to

own about two hundred slaves through inheritance of both Monticello and, later, other property owned by his father-in-law. This would be a point on which Jefferson's political opponents would attack him later in life. Jefferson freed two slaves during his lifetime and five others in his will, and also chose not to try to recapture two others who escaped. He was known to treat his slaves humanely.

In 1772, he married Martha Wayles Skelton, who also came from a prosperous and prominent family. Their first child, Martha, was born the

Jefferson had many accomplishments, with the Louisiana Purchase being one of the most important for the future of the United States. A "Day in the Life" section of the **Monticello: The Home of Thomas Jefferson** site makes for fascinating reading.

EDITOR'S CHOICE

following year. She was the first of six children that the couple would have, but only Martha would outlive Jefferson. Jefferson's wife, Martha, died in 1782.

▷ Brilliant Statesman

Great tragedy in his private life did not deter Jefferson from a tremendously successful public career. Just one year after becoming a lawyer, he was elected to the Virginia colonial legislature. He established himself as an eloquent writer and a supporter of liberty for people of the American colonies when he wrote *A Summary View of the Rights of British America* in 1774. This helped Jefferson get elected the following year to the Continental Congress, a legislative body representing all the British colonies in North America. Disturbed by what it considered unfair impositions placed on the people of the colonies by the British government, the Continental Congress decided to declare independence from Britain in 1776. Because of his reputation as a writer and lover of freedom, Jefferson was chosen to write the document stating why the colonies were breaking from Great Britain. The Declaration of Independence became one of the most famous and influential documents in world history.

During the Revolutionary War, Jefferson served in the newly formed Virginia House of Delegates.

Patriots Benjamin Franklin (left), John Adams (center), and Thomas Jefferson (standing) meet to discuss a draft of the Declaration of Independence. This work of art was created by Jean Leon Gerome.

He composed two pieces of legislation during this time that would prove to be of lasting importance to both Virginia and the newly emergent United States. One was the Statute for Religious Freedom, which allowed for the free practice of all religions and the separation of church and government. The other was the Bill for the More General Diffusion of Knowledge. This called for public elementary education for all children, state-sponsored university systems, and the provision of scholarship funds for highly qualified students. Jefferson also served two years as Virginia's governor.

▶ Diplomacy

Following the success of the Revolutionary War, Jefferson was elected to represent Virginia in the new national Congress, but he only served one year. In 1784, he went to France where he served as trade commissioner. One year later, he succeeded Benjamin Franklin as the United States' principal government representative in France. It was during this time that Jefferson came to be thoroughly familiar with, and appreciative of France and its culture. He also supported the principals of the French Revolution and came to believe that its success would be critical in determining the success of democracy and freedom throughout the world. The fondness Jefferson developed for

France led him to want to avoid war and pursue a peacefully negotiated settlement over the disputed New Orleans and Louisiana territories.

On returning to the United States, Jefferson served in the first presidential Cabinet under George Washington as secretary of state. During this time, he came into conflict with Secretary of the Treasury Alexander Hamilton over the United States' policy toward the conflict in Europe between Great Britain and France. The two men also had differing views on domestic issues. Jefferson felt greater power should be concentrated in state and local governments. Hamilton pushed for a stronger federal government. This was known as the argument between states rights and the rights of the federal government. These differences would eventually lead to the development of the first two political parties in the United States, the Federalists and the Democratic Republicans, also known simply as Democrats.

President Jefferson

Both parties put up candidates in the 1796 presidential election to succeed George Washington. Jefferson barely lost to Federalist John Adams. At that time, the Constitution called for the person finishing second in the presidential election to be vice president. Jefferson assumed that position.

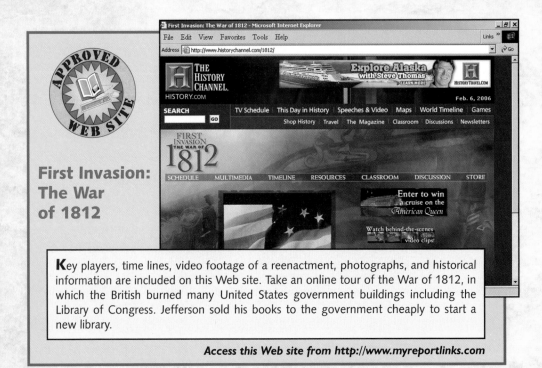

First Invasion: The War of 1812

Key players, time lines, video footage of a reenactment, photographs, and historical information are included on this Web site. Take an online tour of the War of 1812, in which the British burned many United States government buildings including the Library of Congress. Jefferson sold his books to the government cheaply to start a new library.

Access this Web site from http://www.myreportlinks.com

Four years later, Jefferson would reverse the election result and narrowly defeat Adams, becoming the third president of the United States.

This was the first time the presidency passed from one political party to another in the United States, and Jefferson went to great lengths to not upset his opponents. Jefferson took popular measures such as cutting government spending and taxes, and strongly reducing the national debt. These measures, combined with the success of the Louisiana Purchase, made Jefferson so popular with the American people that he was reelected overwhelmingly in 1804, carrying every state but two—Delaware and Connecticut.

Jefferson's public contributions continued after he left the presidency. He sold his extensive book collection to the federal government. This became the start of the Library of Congress, which now holds about 17 million books in its collection. In following his strong commitment to public education, Jefferson founded the University of Virginia in Charlottesville. It opened in 1819. He planned and designed the facility, obtained approval from the state government to build it, oversaw the construction, and served as its first director. Along with writing the Declaration of Independence and the Statute of Virginia for Religious Freedom, the creation of the University of Virginia was one of three accomplishments Jefferson asked to be commemorated for on his tombstone.

Jefferson died on July 4, 1826, exactly fifty years after the signing of the Declaration of Independence. John Adams, his personal friend, political rival, and fellow signatory of the Declaration, died the exact same day, within a few hours of Jefferson.

Toussaint-L'Ouverture: Napoléon Nemesis

Toussaint-L'Ouverture was born into much humbler circumstances than Napoléon Bonaparte or Thomas Jefferson. His father was a slave in the service of a French nobleman, Count de Bréda. The exact date of L'Ouverture's birth is not known.

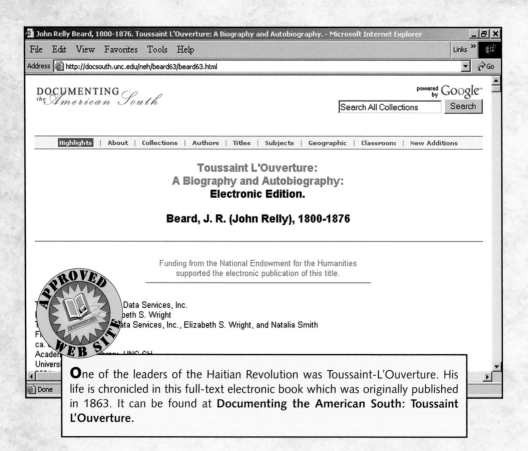

One of the leaders of the Haitian Revolution was Toussaint-L'Ouverture. His life is chronicled in this full-text electronic book which was originally published in 1863. It can be found at **Documenting the American South: Toussaint L'Ouverture.**

It is believed to be either May 20 or November 1, 1743. L'Ouverture showed promise from an early age and was assigned jobs in livestock handling and as Bréda's coachman. Bréda was humane with his slaves and saw L'Ouverture's potential. In spite of laws prohibiting slaves from learning to read and write, Bréda allowed L'Ouverture to receive instruction from a Roman Catholic priest of African descent. L'Ouverture became an avid reader, and exceptionally well informed.

At age thirty-three, L'Ouverture would gain his freedom. He actually took over his own plot of land on which he planted crops and even owned slaves. Nevertheless, he remained committed to principals of liberty and freedom. After the French Revolution, those who had overthrown the monarchists committed themselves to eliminating slavery in all the French colonies. At this point, L'Ouverture decided to join the French Army, which was fighting in Santo Domingo against forces from Britain and Spain. These two nations opposed the new French Revolutionary government. He drove the British out of the port cities that they had occupied after the French Revolution, and even led a French conquest of the Spanish part of the island of Hispaniola, on which Santo Domingo was located. The spectacular triumphs he repeatedly scored against such major powers won him the respect and esteem of the French military as well as most of the people in Santo Domingo. After leading the forces that conquered the island, he was established as the ruler of both the French and Spanish sections.

▶ Betrayal

L'Ouverture drafted a constitution that made him sole ruler of the newly united island. He proclaimed that Santo Domingo would be an independently governed French colony. He professed his loyalty to Napoléon and the French Revolutionary government as long as they honored

▲ This drawing depicts the artist's idea of the scene where Toussaint-L'Ouverture was kidnapped and imprisoned by French forces.

their commitment to ban slavery from their colonies. L'Ouverture suppressed what was limited opposition to his rule with violence, but otherwise ruled kindly. The combination of his stunning military successes and governing style earned him the nickname "the Black Napoléon."

As it were, the real Napoléon did not appreciate L'Ouverture or the comparisons to himself. He led L'Ouverture to believe he would accept his rule and not allow for a return of slavery, but it was typical Napoléon deception. Napoléon had decided that he would restore the plantations that had been taken from the French in the earlier fighting on Santo Domingo to their original owners. He also planned to mislead L'Ouverture. Charles Leclerc was to let L'Ouverture believe he would be allowed to live peacefully on the island if he agreed to cede direct rule back to the French. Of course, once convinced of this, L'Ouverture was abducted and sent to France, where he was imprisoned. He died on April 7, 1803, from neglect and a lack of nourishment.

▶ Inspired by His Death

Resistance to restored French rule on Santo Domingo was not extinguished, as Napoléon had hoped. So revered was L'Ouverture that, when he disappeared and many of his leading generals were captured or killed, there was widespread

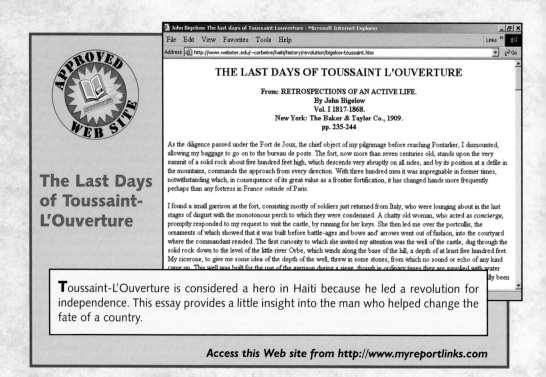

The Last Days of Toussaint-L'Ouverture

THE LAST DAYS OF TOUSSAINT L'OUVERTURE

From: RETROSPECTIONS OF AN ACTIVE LIFE.
By John Bigelow
Vol. I 1817-1868.
New York: The Baker & Taylor Co., 1909.
pp. 235-244

As the diligence passed under the Fort de Joux, the chief object of my pilgrimage before reaching Pontarlier, I dismounted, allowing my baggage to go on to the bureau de poste. The fort, now more than seven centuries old, stands upon the very summit of a solid rock about five hundred feet high, which descends very abruptly on all sides, and by its position at a defile in the mountains, commands the approach from every direction. With three hundred men it was impregnable in former times, notwithstanding which, in consequence of its great value as a frontier fortification, it has changed hands more frequently perhaps than any fortress in France outside of Paris.

I found a small garrison at the fort, consisting mostly of soldiers just returned from Italy, who were lounging about in the last stages of disgust with the monotonous perch to which they were condemned. A chatty old woman, who acted as *concierge*, promptly responded to my request to visit the castle, by running for her keys. She then led me over the portcullis, the ornaments of which showed that it was built before battle-ages and bows and' arrows went out of fashion, into the courtyard where the commandant resided. The first curiosity to which she invited my attention was the well of the castle, dug through the solid rock down to the level of the little river Orbe, which winds along the base of the hill, a depth of at least five hundred feet. My cicerone, to give me some idea of the depth of the well, threw in some stones, from which no sound or echo of any kind came up. This well was built for the use of the garrison during a siege, though in ordinary times they are supplied with water

Toussaint-L'Ouverture is considered a hero in Haiti because he led a revolution for independence. This essay provides a little insight into the man who helped change the fate of a country.

Access this Web site from http://www.myreportlinks.com

fury. When word spread that Napoléon intended to restore slavery to the island, the reaction was more ferociously violent than any attack L'Ouverture had ever led. White landowners and other white citizens were savagely attacked, and cities and towns were set ablaze when the French tried to reassert control. Together with the ravages of yellow fever, the armed opposition so weakened Leclerc's forces that Napoléon had to abandon his plan to have them continue on to New Orleans and Louisiana and occupy those territories.

There were many reasons why Napoléon decided, impulsively as it seemed, to sell the North American territories he had acquired from

Spain rather than defend them. Undoubtedly, the failure of the Santo Domingo military expedition was one that weighed heavily. L'Ouverture and the uprising in Santo Domingo, therefore, has to be credited with playing an important role in swaying Napoléon to sell the territories instead of trying to hold onto them.

Others had tried to lead successful slave rebellions in the past, but none had succeeded before L'Ouverture. His combination of knowledge, personal appeal, and military leadership seem to have been essential factors in creating and sustaining the Santo Domingo uprising. Toussaint-L'Ouverture will never loom as large in world history as Napoléon Bonaparte or Thomas Jefferson. Nevertheless, he clearly stands as an important figure in the history of the Louisiana Purchase.

NEW TERRITORIES JOIN A NATION

In spite of numerous potential pitfalls, New Orleans and the Louisiana Territory both were officially transferred to the possession of the United States by spring 1804. Yet many complications and conflicts over the status and governance of these territories remained. There was uncertainty over their future for the following decade. While the United States and France never went to war over the territories, an international war concerning them did break out between Great Britain and the United States. The War of 1812 played a decisive role in determining that these territories, and others beyond, would fully and permanently become part of the United States.

▷ Legal and Political Issues

The Louisiana Purchase agreement document reached the United States in July 1803. By that time, Napoléon, under continued pressure and persuasion, had begun to express regrets about the agreement. Many French people believed that Louisiana and New Orleans were worth much

▲ A profile of Napoléon Bonaparte.

more than what the United States had paid. Others believed the territories should not have been sold at all. Napoléon's brothers and other members of the ruling elite such as Talleyrand continued their efforts to get the French leader to reverse his decision even after he had approved the purchase. Napoléon seemed increasingly swayed by their efforts as the summer wore on.

Congressional Aid

Word of Napoléon's wavering reached the United States by the time the treaty arrived. Livingston had sent word that the Louisiana Purchase had been unpopular in France, and Napoléon might seize any opportunity to refute it. The treaty had an agreement deadline of October 30. Jefferson certainly welcomed the agreement immediately, but unlike in France, it needed more than the approval of just the head of state. It would need to be approved by the United States Senate. The House of Representatives would also have to vote to provide the money agreed on for the purchase.

Jefferson realized how vital it was to have the United States approve the agreement on time. However, he was also concerned that purchasing land might not be constitutional. Jefferson was a strict constructionist. This meant he felt that any power not expressly granted to the federal government in the United States Constitution did not exist. There was nothing in the Constitution about whether the federal government could acquire new land. Jefferson thought a constitutional amendment would be required to make the Louisiana Purchase legal. Because the amendment process would take longer than the deadline for confirming the agreement allowed, Jefferson was prepared to wait until after the treaty's passage by Congress to seek the amendment.

A majority of Jefferson's presidential Cabinet believed the federal government could legally acquire new lands and territories because the Constitution specified that the government could enter into treaties with other governments. This, they claimed, implied that the federal government could obtain new land under the terms of such a treaty. Jefferson's treasury secretary, Albert Gallatin, put forth the argument that "the existence of the United States as a nation presupposes the power enjoyed by every nation

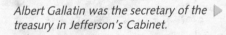

Albert Gallatin was the secretary of the treasury in Jefferson's Cabinet.

of extending their territory by treaties, and the general power given to the President and the Senate in making treaties designates the organs through which the acquisition may be made."[1] Jefferson believed the Louisiana Purchase was of such urgent importance that he reluctantly accepted this argument, even though he had in the past consistently argued against any implied powers in the Constitution. Implied powers are powers the government assumes that are not directly mentioned in the Constitution. In his argument, Gallatin assured Jefferson that the treaty would pass despite some lawmaker's concerns over whether it was legal.

▶ Spanish Opposition

Another complication to the treaty was the strenuous objection to the sale of Louisiana and New Orleans by Spain. France had promised not to turn these territories over to a third party, so Spain claimed the Louisiana Purchase was not valid. So strong was Spanish feeling on this that the Spanish ambassador to the United States, Marquis de Casa Yrujo, wrote two angry letters to Secretary of State Madison. Madison pointed out to Yrujo that the Spanish foreign minister had expressly said in correspondence with the French government that the territories did in fact now belong to France. Still, Yrujo refused to cooperate

▲ A portrait of Jefferson's secretary of state and future president James
Madison. This portrait was done by famous artist Gilbert Stuart.

in the transfer of power to the incoming local French government leader. Jefferson and his Cabinet determined that if in fact the Spanish resisted in handing over Louisiana or New Orleans, the United States would react with military force.

Finalizing the Louisiana Purchase

There were some members of Congress that spoke out strongly against the agreement. Interestingly, some of Jefferson's Federalist opponents, who had often supported the idea of implied powers in the Constitution, now spoke out against them. They claimed the government needed a constitutional amendment to confirm the treaty. Others claimed that the new territories could be made into an American colony but could not become a part of the nation itself.[2] This is what the treaty called for and what Jefferson intended to do with them.

Some members from Northeastern states feared the addition of the territories would produce so many new congressional representatives from western states that the interests of major industrial states such as New York and Massachusetts might be overwhelmed. A few people considered that the United States had spent too much for the territories, even though the cost had only been about five cents per acre after figuring in the interest. These opponents claimed too little was known about the interior of the Louisiana Territory to determine if it was worth the money.

With Jefferson's Democrats holding majorities in both houses of Congress, the treaty was ratified on October 20, 1803. The funds to implement it were approved by the following week. Messengers were immediately deployed to the western territories to deliver news of the treaty's approval. Congress had also authorized Jefferson to raise an army of up to eighty thousand troops and spend $1.5 million on that army if the Spanish resisted turning over the territories. Fears of this subsided when word reached Washington, D.C., that the Spanish had turned over Louisiana to the French on November 30. The French government leader in the territories, Pierre Clémente Laussat, who had arrived by this time, notified the Americans that the Spanish had only a few hundred troops in New Orleans, and these were not at a high level of combat readiness. A large military contingent from the United States would not be necessary to take control of the Louisiana Territory and New Orleans.

▶ Raising the Flag in the New Territory

Among both Spanish and French inhabitants there was resentment and bitterness. When, on December 20, the American flag was raised in a public square in New Orleans, there were cheers and applause from a small group of Americans.

COPYRIGHT 1903 BY

▲ This celebration took place at the St. Louis Cathedral to celebrate the one hundredth anniversary of the Louisiana Purchase.

The rest of the crowd remained silent. Lassaut is said to have cried.

There was much less fanfare when the United States took control of the northern and western parts of the Louisiana Territory on March 9, 1804. This area was so sparsely populated that the French had not bothered to send high-ranking officials there. United States Army Captain Amos Stoddard simply took possession of the area in St. Louis, the largest city in the area.

By the end of that month, the United States Congress had voted to divide the newly acquired lands into two territories. The area around New Orleans and on the opposite side of the Mississippi River, basically the land now comprising the state of Louisiana, was called the Orleans Territory. The more remote and unsettled regions were dubbed Louisiana. Later, when the Orleans Territory became a state in 1812 and was named Louisiana, the remaining territory was renamed Missouri. However, before that came about, there would be yet more tension, conflict, and uncertainty regarding the status and fate of these parcels of land.

Threats of Secession and Revolt

The acquisition of the new territories presented more than one challenge to the unity of the young United States. There had often been speculation that, should the western territories become part of the United States, they would someday separate themselves and form a new nation. Such discussions continued now that the territories had in fact been acquired. European nations that continued to have an interest in the Americas hoped to forge an alliance with such a new emerging nation. Some Europeans encouraged dissenting feelings among the people of the Louisiana territories.

One man who helped encourage secession was Aaron Burr. Burr had been Jefferson's vice president, but the two did not have a good relationship. Their dislike dated back to Jefferson's election. At the time, Burr and Jefferson received the same number of electoral votes. Although Burr knew all along he was only running for vice president, he refused to concede the election. This forced the House of Representatives to have to vote for the president. In what was seen as a fairly unnecessary vote, Jefferson was easily elected president.

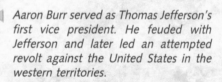

Aaron Burr served as Thomas Jefferson's first vice president. He feuded with Jefferson and later led an attempted revolt against the United States in the western territories.

In 1804, Burr left the vice presidency to run for governor of New York. Burr suffered a decisive defeat to Morgan Lewis, a state judge supported by people loyal to Jefferson. Burr then turned his attention to the newly acquired western territories.

In the first year following the American takeover, Jefferson had created a government for the territories that allowed for no voice at all for the local people. All positions of power were appointed, either directly or indirectly, by the president. This led to widespread dissatisfaction, and in December 1804, a group of three delegates from Louisiana traveled to Washington to address their complaints to Jefferson. These delegates were met with great sympathy by Burr. He heard from the delegates about Mexicans in New Orleans seeking aid for an attempted uprising against Spanish rule in that country. Learning this, Burr came up with a scheme to start a new nation in central North America that would include both the Louisiana and Missouri territories as well as Mexico.

A Selfish Plan

Burr figured that if he could lead a successful uprising against Spain in Mexico and take control of that country's prosperous mines, he could also exploit discontent in the western American territories. He thought he could convince those people to join a

The first chief justice of the Supreme Court, John Marshall.

new nation that would combine their territory with the enormous wealth provided by Mexico's mines.

In pursuing this goal, Burr conspired with the chief commander of the United States Army, General James Wilkinson. Wilkinson had a history of corruption, having previously accepted money from the Spanish to spy on his fellow Americans. He stood ready to put the troops he commanded into a revolutionary war in Mexico.

Burr also elicited support from the British ambassador to the United States, Anthony Merry, who liked the idea of a new nation independent of the United States. Such a nation could be a major trading partner with Great Britain's large colony of Canada, or perhaps even become part of the British Empire. Merry sought to get his government to commit to sending a squadron to the mouth of the Mississippi to prevent any troops sent by Jefferson from stopping Wilkinson and Burr in their venture.

▷ Burr Gets Caught

Merry's attempts would fail. Great Britain had gone to war with France and faced too stiff a military challenge in that conflict to spare any troops or supplies. Also, Burr's plans had not been kept secret since he had publicly campaigned in the western territories to help build support for the venture. Without British support and the element of surprise to work with, General Wilkinson backed out of the plan. He revealed Burr's role in it as a way to win the favor of both the United States and Spanish governments. Wilkinson ordered the arrests of those Burr had sent to New Orleans, and Jefferson ordered Burr and his other followers arrested as well.

Burr and a group of armed followers were apprehended in January 1807. Burr was tried for treason, but Chief Justice of the Supreme Court John Marshall found that Burr's actions did not fit the definition of treason in the U.S. Constitution. He was found not guilty. Yet he became so widely and deeply resented by Americans that he had to flee after his trial. He lived in Europe for several years to avoid the rage of those who felt he had betrayed his country. Eventually, he returned to New York.

▶ Exploration and Expansion

Unlike European nations, the United States bordered the Louisiana Territory, and it was much easier for that country to explore its vast wilderness. Even before the Louisiana Purchase was completed, Jefferson planned an expedition into the territory. Named to head the expedition were two army officers, Captain Meriwether Lewis and Lieutenant William Clark. They and forty followers comprised the Corps of Discovery, which was assigned by Jefferson to survey the territory and the land beyond and gather as much information on the geography, ecology, and inhabitants in the region as possible. Like other explorers, Lewis and Clark also hoped to find a water passage through North America to the Pacific.

The Corps of Discovery failed to find this passageway, and for the first time it was concluded that none existed in central North America. Otherwise, the voyage, which lasted from 1804 until 1806, was a tremendous success. The corps produced the first quality maps of the territory

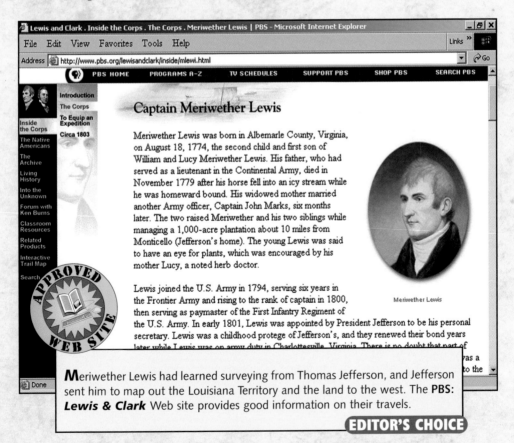

Meriwether Lewis had learned surveying from Thomas Jefferson, and Jefferson sent him to map out the Louisiana Territory and the land to the west. The **PBS: Lewis & Clark** Web site provides good information on their travels.

EDITOR'S CHOICE

and returned with a mass of information on the area's wildlife, topography, climate, and American Indian populations. Lewis and Clark successfully navigated to the Pacific coast along a route that would become known as the Oregon Trail.

▷ Findings of Lewis & Clark

As a result of the wealth of information gained by the Corps of Discovery, the Lewis and Clark expedition took on legendary fame. Soon thousands of travelers were following the route the explorers took westward, settling new lands and starting new towns and villages. The Lewis and Clark team had reported that there were vast fertile lands and pleasant climates in the western areas. The massive movement of Americans westward that had begun even before the Revolutionary War continued and grew.

Initially, for the most part, the new American settlers lived at peace with the American Indians. William Clark had developed ties with many

◁ In this dramatic image painted by famous landscape artist William Henry Jackson, Sacajawea is being reunited with her Shoshone people. Sacajawea is perhaps the most famous member of Lewis & Clark's Corps of Discovery.

William Clark, along with Meriwether Lewis, led the Corps of Discovery.

American Indian tribes in his lifetime and had become well versed in and appreciative of their culture and customs. The Great Plains region was an area particularly important to the American Indians, but the first American immigrants to the west largely passed these areas by, considering them undesirable for living. Nevertheless, some conflicts did break out. These increased as greater numbers of new settlers came, and many of them moved onto the Great Plains and other important American Indian dwelling areas.

The War of 1812

American territorial expansion did not just provoke conflict with American Indians. To the south of Louisiana, the United States and Spain disputed territory along the eastern bank of the Mississippi River and the shoreline of the Gulf of Mexico. This conflict had begun almost immediately after the Louisiana Purchase was approved. Once again, the United States tried to negotiate with Spain and purchase Florida just as it had Louisiana, but these attempts failed. Tensions worsened in 1810. In response to an uprising by Americans within Florida, United States President James Madison ordered a section of western Florida seized by force.

Great Britain was also angry because large numbers of American fur trappers were moving

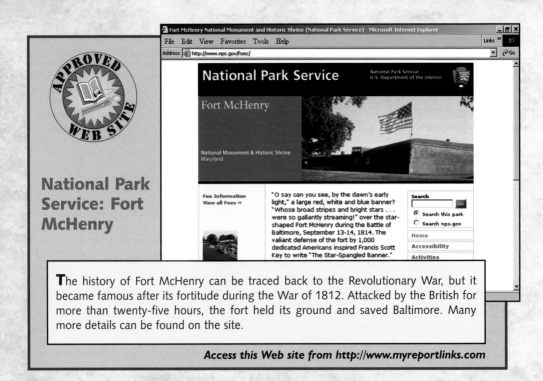

National Park
Service: Fort
McHenry

The history of Fort McHenry can be traced back to the Revolutionary War, but it became famous after its fortitude during the War of 1812. Attacked by the British for more than twenty-five hours, the fort held its ground and saved Baltimore. Many more details can be found on the site.

Access this Web site from http://www.myreportlinks.com

into the northern and western woods that had been traversed by Lewis and Clark. The British had a virtual monopoly on fur trading in these woodlands and resented losing any of it to the Americans.

These two countries united against the United States in the years leading up to the War of 1812, which the United States declared against Great Britain. Once again American Indians were attacking Americans traveling and settling in the western territories, this time with encouragement from the British. The British still hoped to encourage the western territories to break from the United States and to possibly even unite this area with Canada to the north. Additionally, Great Britain had emerged as the world's leading military power in the early 1800s. It saw the new, fast-growing United States as a possible long-term rival. Britain supported Spain in its dispute with the United States over Florida. Many Americans believed they should seize Florida immediately by force.

The War of 1812 lasted two years and included widespread ferocious and devastating combat action. The city of Washington, D.C., was invaded and occupied by the British, and several important public buildings, including the White House, were

The Cabildo

The Battle of New Orleans

The fighting in Louisiana was really a series of battles *for* New Orleans, lasting from December 1814 through

Learn about the Battle of New Orleans from this educational site. The battle was a key moment in American history because if the British had taken control of New Orleans they would have controlled the Mississippi River. Learn more from **The Cabildo: The Battle of New Orleans.**

EDITOR'S CHOICE

▲ *Although the port of New Orleans may have been the most lucrative part of the Louisiana Purchase, many other parts of the Louisiana Territory have been important. Here wagon trains retrace the route of the Oregon Trail through Nebraska.*

badly damaged. Probably the most famous battle of the war was the Battle of New Orleans. Oddly enough, it took place weeks after the war ended in a peace settlement in December 1814. Because news of the peace had to be carried by messenger, it had not yet reached either British or American troops around New Orleans the following January. In the Battle of New Orleans, American Colonel

Andrew Jackson gained fame by routing the British. He used clever strategy and a strong familiarity with the area's geography and terrain. In the battle, only thirteen Americans were killed while the British lost seven hundred. Jackson became the seventh United States president in 1829.

Americans Gain Preeminence

The Treaty of Ghent between Great Britain and the United States settled the War of 1812. It amounted to no new territorial gain for either country. Even still, by standing up to Great Britain, the United States further established itself. American movement and expansion continued and grew, and was mostly unaffected. Florida became part of the United States in 1819. Many other new western states followed Louisiana's admission. Starting with Missouri in 1821, fourteen other states were formed in the next ninety-one years either wholly or partly from land gained in the Louisiana Purchase. Using the precedent set by the Louisiana Purchase, new territories were purchased from Spain, Great Britain, and Russia. This provided the United States with its current borders. The westward expansion of the United States, so central to the nation's growth and history, was clearly greatly dependent on the Louisiana Purchase and its successful execution.

Report Links

The Internet sites described below can be accessed at
http://www.myreportlinks.com

▶**Primary Documents in American History: Louisiana Purchase**
Editor's Choice This is the Library of Congress Web site for the Louisiana Purchase.

▶**French Louisiana, 1682–1803**
Editor's Choice The French Ministry of Culture presents this Web site on Louisiana.

▶**The Cabildo: The Battle of New Orleans**
Editor's Choice A Louisiana State Museum Web page on the final battle of the War of 1812.

▶**Louisiana's Old State Capitol Presents "The Louisiana Purchase Exhibit"**
Editor's Choice Louisiana Department of State Web site on the history of the famous Louisiana Purchase.

▶**PBS: *Lewis & Clark***
Editor's Choice Visit this PBS site to learn more about Lewis and Clark.

▶**Monticello: The Home of Thomas Jefferson**
Editor's Choice The life and times of Jefferson set against the backdrop of his estate.

▶**The American History Company: The Jeffersonian Republicans, 1801–1812**
Read about American politics during the early 1800s.

▶**Digital History: Native American Voices**
This site looks at the plight of American Indians during the 1800s.

▶**Documenting the American South: Toussaint-L'Ouverture**
Learn more about the hero of Santo Domingo.

▶**The Explorers: Louis Jolliet**
This Canadian Museum of Civilization Web site looks at explorer Louis Jolliet.

▶**First Invasion: The War of 1812**
The History Channel brings us the War of 1812.

▶**French Leaders**
Take a look inside the important leaders of Napoleon's empire.

▶**Haiti Archives: The Haitian Revolution**
This is an overview of the thirteen-year revolution for independence in Haiti.

▶**History and Culture of the Lower Mississippi Delta**
This National Park Service site looks at the history of the Lower Mississippi Delta.

▶**The James Madison Center: Madison Archives**
James Madison University offers this Web site about its founder.

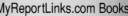
The Internet sites described below can be accessed at
http://www.myreportlinks.com

▶**James Monroe**
Visit the home of James Monroe in Virginia.

▶**The Last Days of Toussaint-L'Ouverture**
An article on how Toussaint-L'Ouverture spent his last days in prison.

▶**The Library of Congress: France in America**
This Library of Congress site provides an overview of the French presence in America.

▶*Life of Thomas Jefferson*
Electronic version of B. L. Rayner's 1834 book on Jefferson is available here.

▶**The Louisiana Purchase: A Heritage Explored**
Louisiana State University Libraries created this portal site for the Louisiana Purchase.

▶**Napoléon: An Intimate Portrait**
Learn about Napoléon from this traveling museum exhibit.

▶**Napoleon.org**
Learn almost all you can about Napoléon from this online resource.

▶**Napoleonic Guide**
This is a comprehensive resource for information on Napoléon.

▶**National Park Service: Fort McHenry**
The National Park Service celebrates Fort McHenry, a pivotal War of 1812 site.

▶**An Outline of American History: Westward Expansion and Regional Differences**
The growth of the United States is outlined on this Web site.

▶**Spanish Exploration and Conquest of Native America**
This site offers an overview of Spain's exploration of the New World.

▶**University of Mary Washington: The Negotiator: Robert Livingston**
Learn more about Robert Livingston from this article.

▶**University: Michigan State: French Explorers**
This Michigan State University sites provides an overview of early French explorers.

▶**The University of Texas at Austin: TSHA Online: La Salle Expedition**
A brief look at the history of the La Salle expedition.

▶*The World Factbook:* Haiti
This is an overview of Haiti, formerly part of Santo Domingo.

arbitrary—Depending on the whim or decisions of one particular person.

buffer zone—A neutral or safe area between two rival nations.

cede—To turn over the rights to something, usually by treaty.

colonize—To establish settlements of people in a foreign land, usually for economic gain.

cunning—Crafty and insightful.

diplomat—A person whose job it is to negotiate for his or her nation with other nations.

envoy—A person chosen to represent a government in dealings with another.

expedition—A journey, or group of travelers making a journey, with a specific reason in mind.

frontier dwellers—Those that live at the edges of a country's borders, usually by unexplored territory.

fourfold—Four times the original amount.

immunity—To be unaffected by a disease or illness.

missionary—A religious servant whose goal it is to convert other people to his or her religion.

Mississippians—Ancient people who were native to the Mississippi River valley. Their descendants became parts of the Chickasaw, Choctaw, and Natchez tribes, among others.

Manifest Destiny—Belief that it was the destiny of the United States to have its borders span from the Atlantic to the Pacific oceans.

monarchy—Government ruled by a king or queen.

Napoleonic Code—A rule of law where judges decide cases based on the laws of the legislature rather than using the example of past legal decisions. The state of Louisiana still follows Napoleonic Code. It is the only state that does so.

plunder—To raid violently and steal from a person or people.

secession—The act of leaving a union or breaking away from a country.

vagrant—A wanderer or bum with no established residence.

venture—(verb) To travel to, or explore a region.

wrangled—Negotiated or argued over.

yellow fever—An infectious disease caused by the yellow-fever mosquito.

Chapter 1. On the Brink of War

1. Fred Israel, ed., *Major Presidential Decisions* (New York: Chelsea House, 1980), pp. 36–37.

2. Quoted in Thomas Fleming, *The Louisiana Purchase* (Hoboken, N.J.: John Wiley & Sons, 2003), p. 99.

3. Fleming, p. 117.

Chapter 2. Exploration and Establishment of the Louisiana Territory

1. Lynda Shaffer, "Mississippians," *Encyclopedia of North American Indians,* n.d., <http://college.hmco.com/history/readerscomp/naind/html/na_022800_mississippia.htm> (February 9, 2006).

2. Marshall Sprague, *So Vast, So Beautiful a Land: Louisiana and the Purchase* (Boston: Little Brown and Company, 1974), pp. 9–12.

3. The Texas Historical Commission, "Life & Times of La Salle," 2002, <http://www.thc.state.tx.us/lasalle/laslife.html> (February 9, 2006).

4. Alexander DeConde, *This Affair of Louisiana* (New York: Charles Scribner's Sons, 1976), p. 14.

Chapter 3. Wrangling Over Spanish Louisiana

1. Stephen E. Ambrose, *Undaunted Courage: Meriwether Lewis, Thomas Jefferson, and the Opening of the American West* (New York: Simon and Schuster, 1996), pp. 71–72.

2. Thomas Fleming, *The Louisiana Purchase* (Hoboken, N.J.: John Wiley & Sons, 2003), p. 89.

3. Peter Hicks, "Louisians: To Have and to Have Not . . . " *Napoleon.org,* n.d., <http://www.napoleon.org/en/reading_room/articles/files/Louisiana_hicks.asp> (February 9, 2006).

Chapter 4. Making the Deal: France and America

1. Fawn M. Brodie, *Thomas Jefferson: An Intimate History* (New York: W.W. Norton & Company, 1974), p. 344.

2. Ibid., p. 341.

3. Thomas Fleming, *The Louisiana Purchase* (Hoboken, NJ: John Wiley & Sons, 2003), p. 77.

Chapter 5. Pivotal Players in the Louisiana Purchase

1. Michael Hart, *The 100: A Ranking of the Most Influential Persons in History* (New York: Gallahad Books, 1978), p. 205.

2. Thomas Jefferson, "To the Governor of Virginia (James Monroe) Washington, Nov. 24, 1801," *The Letters of Thomas Jefferson: 1743–1826,* March 6, 2003, <http://www.let.rug.nl/usa/P/tj3/writings/brf/jefl142.htm> (February 9, 2006).

Chapter 6. New Territories Join a Nation

1. Fred Israel, ed., *Major Presidential Decisions* (New York: Chelsea House, 1990), p. 162.

2. Walter LaFeber, *The American Age: U.S. Foreign Policy at Home and Abroad – 1750 to the Present,* 2nd edition (New York: W.W. Norton & Company, 1994), p. 58.

Alagna, Magdalena. *The Louisiana Purchase: Expanding America's Boundaries*. New York: Rosen Publishing Group, 2004.

Burgan, Michael. *The Louisiana Purchase*. Minneapolis, Minn.: Compass Point Books, 2002.

Corrick, James A. *The Louisiana Purchase*. San Diego, Calif.: Lucent, 2001.

Davenport, John. *Louisiana Territory*. Philadelphia: Chelsea House Publishers, 2005.

Faber, Harold. *Lewis and Clark: From Ocean to Ocean*. Tarrytown, N.Y.: Benchmark/Marshall Cavendish, 2002.

Jaffe, Elizabeth D. *The Louisiana Purchase*. Mankato, Minn.: Bridgestone Books, 2002.

Kent, Zachary. *James Madison: Creating a Nation*. Berkeley Heights, N.J.: Enslow Publishers, Inc., 2004.

Obstfeld, Raymond and Loretta, ed. *Napoleon Bonaparte*. San Diego, Calif.: Greenhaven Press, 2001.

Reiter, Chris. *Thomas Jefferson*. Berkeley Heights, N.J.: MyReportLinks.com Books, 2002.

Roop, Peter. *Louisiana Purchase*. New York: Aladdin Paperbacks, 2004.

Staeger, Rob. *The Journey of Lewis and Clark: How the Corps of Discovery Explored the Louisiana Purchase, Reached the Pacific Ocean, and Returned Safely*. Philadelphia: Mason Crest, 2003.